Spencer's Decimal Currency
Ready Reckoner

JOHN SPENCER & CO. (Publishers) LIMITED.
131 BRACKENBURY ROAD, LONDON, W6.

First Printing April 1969
Second Printing May 1969
Third Printing November 1969
Fourth Printing August 1970
Fifth Printing January 1971
Sixth Printing January 1971
Seventh Printing February 1971
Eighth Printing March 1971
Ninth Printing July 1972
Tenth Printing July 1975

Every care has been taken to ensure accuracy throughout this
Ready Reckoner. Neither the Publishers nor the Printers can
admit liability for any loss incurred through misprint or other
circumstances.

Made and printed in Great Britain by
Hunt Barnard Printing Ltd., Aylesbury, Bucks.
SBN 85436 000 X

CONTENTS

½ NEW PENCE

	£.np.		£.np.		£.np.		£.np.
1	$\frac{1}{2}$	27	$13\frac{1}{2}$	53	$26\frac{1}{2}$	79	$39\frac{1}{2}$
2	1	28	14	54	27	80	40
3	$1\frac{1}{2}$	29	$14\frac{1}{2}$	55	$27\frac{1}{2}$	81	$40\frac{1}{2}$
4	2	30	15	56	28	82	41
5	$2\frac{1}{2}$	31	$15\frac{1}{2}$	57	$28\frac{1}{2}$	83	$41\frac{1}{2}$
6	3	32	16	58	29	84	42
7	$3\frac{1}{2}$	33	$16\frac{1}{2}$	59	$29\frac{1}{2}$	85	$42\frac{1}{2}$
8	4	34	17	60	30	86	43
9	$4\frac{1}{2}$	35	$17\frac{1}{2}$	61	$30\frac{1}{2}$	87	$43\frac{1}{2}$
10	5	36	18	62	31	88	44
11	$5\frac{1}{2}$	37	$18\frac{1}{2}$	63	$31\frac{1}{2}$	89	$44\frac{1}{2}$
12	6	38	19	64	32	90	45
13	$6\frac{1}{2}$	39	$19\frac{1}{2}$	65	$32\frac{1}{2}$	91	$45\frac{1}{2}$
14	7	40	20	66	33	92	46
15	$7\frac{1}{2}$	41	$20\frac{1}{2}$	67	$33\frac{1}{2}$	93	$46\frac{1}{2}$
16	8	42	21	68	34	94	47
17	$8\frac{1}{2}$	43	$21\frac{1}{2}$	69	$34\frac{1}{2}$	95	$47\frac{1}{2}$
18	9	44	22	70	35	96	48
19	$9\frac{1}{2}$	45	$22\frac{1}{2}$	71	$35\frac{1}{2}$	97	$48\frac{1}{2}$
20	10	46	23	72	36	98	49
21	$10\frac{1}{2}$	47	$23\frac{1}{2}$	73	$36\frac{1}{2}$	99	$49\frac{1}{2}$
22	11	48	24	74	37	100	50
23	$11\frac{1}{2}$	49	$24\frac{1}{2}$	75	$37\frac{1}{2}$	200	1.00
24	12	50	25	76	38	400	2.00
25	$12\frac{1}{2}$	51	$25\frac{1}{2}$	77	$38\frac{1}{2}$	600	3.00
26	13	52	26	78	39	1000	5.00

	£.np.		£.np.		£.np.		£.np.
1	1	27	27	53	53	79	79
2	2	28	28	54	54	80	80
3	3	29	29	55	55	81	81
4	4	30	30	56	56	82	82
5	5	31	31	57	57	83	83
6	6	32	32	58	58	84	84
7	7	33	33	59	59	85	85
8	8	34	34	60	60	86	86
9	9	35	35	61	61	87	87
10	10	36	36	62	62	88	88
11	11	37	37	63	63	89	89
12	12	38	38	64	64	90	90
13	13	39	39	65	65	91	91
14	14	40	40	66	66	92	92
15	15	41	41	67	67	93	93
16	16	42	42	68	68	94	94
17	17	43	43	69	69	95	95
18	18	44	44	70	70	96	96
19	19	45	45	71	71	97	97
20	20	46	46	72	72	98	98
21	21	47	47	73	73	99	99
22	22	48	48	74	74	100	1.00
23	23	49	49	75	75	200	2.00
24	24	50	50	76	76	400	4.00
25	25	51	51	77	77	600	6.00
26	26	52	52	78	78	1000	10.00

1½ NEW PENCE

	£.np.		£.np.		£.np.		£.np.
1	1½	27	40½	53	79½	79	1.18½
2	3	28	42	54	81	80	1.20
3	4½	29	43½	55	82½	81	1.21½
4	6	30	45	56	84	82	1.23
5	7½	31	46½	57	85½	83	1.24½
6	9	32	48	58	87	84	1.26
7	10½	33	49½	59	88½	85	1.27½
8	12	34	51	60	90	86	1.29
9	13½	35	52½	61	91½	87	1.30½
10	15	36	54	62	93	88	1.32
11	16½	37	55½	63	94½	89	1.33½
12	18	38	57	64	96	90	1.35
13	19½	39	58½	65	97½	91	1.36½
14	21	40	60	66	99	92	1.38
15	22½	41	61½	67	1.00½	93	1.39½
16	24	42	63	68	1.02	94	1.41
17	25½	43	64½	69	1.03½	95	1.42½
18	27	44	66	70	1.05	96	1.44
19	28½	45	67½	71	1.06½	97	1.45½
20	30	46	69	72	1.08	98	1.47
21	31½	47	70½	73	1.09½	99	1.48½
22	33	48	72	74	1.11	100	1.50
23	34½	49	73½	75	1.12½	200	3.00
24	36	50	75	76	1.14	400	6.00
25	37½	51	76½	77	1.15½	600	9.00
26	39	52	78	78	1.17	1000	15.00

2 NEW PENCE

	£.np.		£.np.		£.np.		£.np.
1	2	27	54	53	1.06	79	1.58
2	4	28	56	54	1.08	80	1.60
3	6	29	58	55	1.10	81	1.62
4	8	30	60	56	1.12	82	1.64
5	10	31	62	57	1.14	83	1.66
6	12	32	64	58	1.16	84	1.68
7	14	33	66	59	1.18	85	1.70
8	16	34	68	60	1.20	86	1.72
9	18	35	70	61	1.22	87	1.74
10	20	36	72	62	1.24	88	1.76
11	22	37	74	63	1.26	89	1.78
12	24	38	76	64	1.28	90	1.80
13	26	39	78	65	1.30	91	1.82
14	28	40	80	66	1.32	92	1.84
15	30	41	82	67	1.34	93	1.86
16	32	42	84	68	1.36	94	1.88
17	34	43	86	69	1.38	95	1.90
18	36	44	88	70	1.40	96	1.92
19	38	45	90	71	1.42	97	1.94
20	40	46	92	72	1.44	98	1.96
21	42	47	94	73	1.46	99	1.98
22	44	48	96	74	1.48	100	2.00
23	46	49	98	75	1.50	200	4.00
24	48	50	1.00	76	1.52	400	8.00
25	50	51	1.02	77	1.54	600	12.00
26	52	52	1.04	78	1.56	1000	20.00

2½ NEW PENCE

	£.np.		£.np.		£.np.		£.np.
1	2½	27	67½	53	1.32½	79	1.97½
2	5	28	70	54	1.35	80	2.00
3	7½	29	72½	55	1.37½	81	2.02½
4	10	30	75	56	1.40	82	2.05
5	12½	31	77½	57	1.42½	83	2.07½
6	15	32	80	58	1.45	84	2.10
7	17½	33	82½	59	1.47½	85	2.12½
8	20	34	85	60	1.50	86	2.15
9	22½	35	87½	61	1.52½	87	2.17½
10	25	36	90	62	1.55	88	2.20
11	27½	37	92½	63	1.57½	89	2.22½
12	30	38	95	64	1.60	90	2.25
13	32½	39	97½	65	1.62½	91	2.27½
14	35	40	1.00	66	1.65	92	2.30
15	37½	41	1.02½	67	1.67½	93	2.32½
16	40	42	1.05	68	1.70	94	2.35
17	42½	43	1.07½	69	1.72½	95	2.37½
18	45	44	1.10	70	1.75	96	2.40
19	47½	45	1.12½	71	1.77½	97	2.42½
20	50	46	1.15	72	1.80	98	2.45
21	52½	47	1.17½	73	1.82½	99	2.47½
22	55	48	1.20	74	1.85	100	2.50
23	57½	49	1.22½	75	1.87½	200	5.00
24	60	50	1.25	76	1.90	400	10.00
25	62½	51	1.27½	77	1.92½	600	15.00
26	65	52	1.30	78	1.95	1000	25.00

3 NEW PENCE

	£.np.		£.np.		£.np.		£.np.
1	3	27	81	53	1.59	79	2.37
2	6	28	.84	54	1.62	80	2.40
3	9	29	87	55	1.65	81	2.43
4	12	30	90	56	1.68	82	2.46
5	15	31	93	57	1.71	83	2.49
6	18	32	96	58	1.74	84	2.52
7	21	33	99	59	1.77	85	2.55
8	24	34	1.02	60	1.80	86	2.58
9	27	35	1.05	61	1.83	87	2.61
10	30	36	1.08	62	1.86	88	2.64
11	33	37	1.11	63	1.89	89	2.67
12	36	38	1.14	64	1.92	90	2.70
13	39	39	1.17	65	1.95	91	2.73
14	42	40	1.20	66	1.98	92	2.76
15	45	41	1.23	67	2.01	93	2.79
16	48	42	1.26	68	2.04	94	2.82
17	51	43	1.29	69	2.07	95	2.85
18	54	44	1.32	70	2.10	96	2.88
19	57	45	1.35	71	2.13	97	2.91
20	60	46	1.38	72	2.16	98	2.94
21	63	47	1.41	73	2.19	99	2.97
22	66	48	1.44	74	2.22	100	3.00
23	69	49	1.47	75	2.25	200	6.00
24	72	50	1.50	76	2.28	400	12.00
25	75	51	1.53	77	2.31	600	18.00
26	78	52	1.56	78	2.34	1000	30.00

	£.np.		£.np.		£.np.		£.np.
1	3½	27	94½	53	1.85½	79	2.76½
2	7	28	98	54	1.89	80	2.80
3	10½	29	1.01½	55	1.92½	81	2.83½
4	14	30	1.05	56	1.96	82	2.87
5	17½	31	1.08½	57	1.99½	83	2.90½
6	21	32	1.12	58	2.03	84	2.94
7	24½	33	1.15½	59	2.06½	85	2.97½
8	28	34	1.19	60	2.10	86	3.01
9	31½	35	1.22½	61	2.13½	87	3.04½
10	35	36	1.26	62	2.17	88	3.08
11	38½	37	1.29½	63	2.20½	89	3.11½
12	42	38	1.33	64	2.24	90	3.15
13	45½	39	1.36½	65	2.27½	91	3.18½
14	49	40	1.40	66	2.31	92	3.22
15	52½	41	1.43½	67	2.34½	93	3.25½
16	56	42	1.47	68	2.38	94	3.29
17	59½	43	1.50½	69	2.41½	95	3.32½
18	63	44	1.54	70	2.45	96	3.36
19	66½	45	1.57½	71	2.48½	97	3.39½
20	70	46	1.61	72	2.52	98	3.43
21	73½	47	1.64½	73	2.55½	99	3.46½
22	77	48	1.68	74	2.59	100	3.50
23	80½	49	1.71½	75	2.62½	200	7.00
24	84	50	1.75	76	2.66	400	14.00
25	87½	51	1.78½	77	2.69½	600	21.00
26	91	52	1.82	78	2.73	1000	35.00

4 NEW PENCE

	£.np.		£.np.		£.np.		£.np.
1	4	27	1.08	53	2.12	79	3.16
2	8	28	1.12	54	2.16	80	3.20
3	12	29	1.16	55	2.20	81	3.24
4	16	30	1.20	56	2.24	82	3.28
5	20	31	1.24	57	2.28	83	3.32
6	24	32	1.28	58	2.32	84	3.36
7	28	33	1.32	59	2.36	85	3.40
8	32	34	1.36	60	2.40	86	3.44
9	36	35	1.40	61	2.44	87	3.48
10	40	36	1.44	62	2.48	88	3.52
11	44	37	1.48	63	2.52	89	3.56
12	48	38	1.52	64	2.56	90	3.60
13	52	39	1.56	65	2.60	91	3.64
14	56	40	1.60	66	2.64	92	3.68
15	60	41	1.64	67	2.68	93	3.72
16	64	42	1.68	68	2.72	94	3.76
17	68	43	1.72	69	2.76	95	3.80
18	72	44	1.76	70	2.80	96	3.84
19	76	45	1.80	71	2.84	97	3.88
20	80	46	1.84	72	2.88	98	3.92
21	84	47	1.88	73	2.92	99	3.96
22	88	48	1.92	74	2.96	100	4.00
23	92	49	1.96	75	3.00	200	8.00
24	96	50	2.00	76	3.04	400	16.00
25	1.00	51	2.04	77	3.08	600	24.00
26	1.04	52	2.08	78	3.12	1000	40.00

4½ NEW PENCE

	£.np.		£.np.		£.np.		£.np.
1	4½	27	1.21½	53	2.38½	79	3.55½
2	9	28	1.26	54	2.43	80	3.60
3	13½	29	1.30½	55	2.47½	81	3.64½
4	18	30	1.35	56	2.52	82	3.69
5	22½	31	1.39½	57	2.56½	83	3.73½
6	27	32	1.44	58	2.61	84	3.78
7	31½	33	1.48½	59	2.65½	85	3.82½
8	36	34	1.53	60	2.70	86	3.87
9	40½	35	1.57½	61	2.74½	87	3.91½
10	45	36	1.62	62	2.79	88	3.96
11	49½	37	1.66½	63	2.83½	89	4.00½
12	54	38	1.71	64	2.88	90	4.05
13	58½	39	1.75½	65	2.92½	91	4.09½
14	63	40	1.80	66	2.97	92	4.14
15	67½	41	1.84½	67	3.01½	93	4.18½
16	72	42	1.89	68	3.06	94	4.23
17	76½	43	1.93½	69	3.10½	95	4.27½
18	81	44	1.98	70	3.15	96	4.32
19	85½	45	2.02½	71	3.19½	97	4.36½
20	90	46	2.07	72	3.24	98	4.41
21	94½	47	2.11½	73	3.28½	99	4.45½
22	99	48	2.16	74	3.33	100	4.50
23	1.03½	49	2.20½	75	3.37½	200	9.00
24	1.08	50	2.25	76	3.42	400	18.00
25	1.12½	51	2.29½	77	3.46½	600	27.00
26	1.17	52	2.34	78	3.51	1000	45.00

5 NEW PENCE

	£.np.		£.np.		£.np.		£.np.
1	5	27	1.35	53	2.65	79	3.95
2	10	28	1.40	54	2.70	80	4.00
3	15	29	1.45	55	2.75	81	4.05
4	20	30	1.50	56	2.80	82	4.10
5	25	31	1.55	57	2.85	83	4.15
6	30	32	1.60	58	2.90	84	4.20
7	35	33	1.65	59	2.95	85	4.25
8	40	34	1.70	60	3.00	86	4.30
9	45	35	1.75	61	3.05	87	4.35
10	50	36	1.80	62	3.10	88	4.40
11	55	37	1.85	63	3.15	89	4.45
12	60	38	1.90	64	3.20	90	4.50
13	65	39	1.95	65	3.25	91	4.55
14	70	40	2.00	66	3.30	92	4.60
15	75	41	2.05	67	3.35	93	4.65
16	80	42	2.10	68	3.40	94	4.70
17	85	43	2.15	69	3.45	95	4.75
18	90	44	2.20	70	3.50	96	4.80
19	95	45	2.25	71	3.55	97	4.85
20	1.00	46	2.30	72	3.60	98	4.90
21	1.05	47	2.35	73	3.65	99	4.95
22	1.10	48	2.40	74	3.70	100	5.00
23	1.15	49	2.45	75	3.75	200	10.00
24	1.20	50	2.50	76	3.80	400	20.00
25	1.25	51	2.55	77	3.85	600	30.00
26	1.30	52	2.60	78	3.90	1000	50.00

5½ NEW PENCE

	£.np.		£.np.		£.np.		£.np.
1	5½	27	1.48½	53	2.91½	79	4.34½
2	11	28	1.54	54	2.97	80	4.40
3	16½	29	1.59½	55	3.02½	81	4.45½
4	22	30	1.65	56	3.08	82	4.51
5	27½	31	1.70½	57	3.13½	83	4.56½
6	33	32	1.76	58	3.19	84	4.62
7	38½	33	1.81½	59	3.24½	85	4.67½
8	44	34	1.87	60	3.30	86	4.73
9	49½	35	1.92½	61	3.35½	87	4.78½
10	55	36	1.98	62	3.41	88	4.84
11	60½	37	2.03½	63	3.46½	89	4.89½
12	66	38	2.09	64	3.52	90	4.95
13	71½	39	2.14½	65	3.57½	91	5.00½
14	77	40	2.20	66	3.63	92	5.06
15	82½	41	2.25½	67	3.68½	93	5.11½
16	88	42	2.31	68	3.74	94	5.17
17	93½	43	2.36½	69	3.79½	95	5.22½
18	99	44	2.42	70	3.85	96	5.28
19	1.04½	45	2.47½	71	3.90½	97	5.33½
20	1.10	46	2.53	72	3.96	98	5.39
21	1.15½	47	2.58½	73	4.01½	99	5.44½
22	1.21	48	2.64	74	4.07	100	5.50
23	1.26½	49	2.69½	75	4.12½	200	11.00
24	1.32	50	2.75	76	4.18	400	22.00
25	1.37½	51	2.80½	77	4.23½	600	33.00
26	1.43	52	2.86	78	4.29	1000	55.00

6 NEW PENCE

	£.np.		£.np.		£ np		£.np.
1	6	27	1.62	53	3.18	79	4.74
2	12	28	1.68	54	3.24	80	4.80
3	18	29	1.74	55	3.30	81	4.86
4	24	30	1.80	56	3.36	82	4.92
5	30	31	1.86	57	3.42	83	4.98
6	36	32	1.92	58	3.48	84	5.04
7	42	33	1.98	59	3.54	85	5.10
8	48	34	2.04	60	3.60	86	5.16
9	54	35	2.10	61	3.66	87	5.22
10	60	36	2.16	62	3.72	88	5.28
11	66	37	2.22	63	3.78	89	5.34
12	72	38	2.28	64	3.84	90	5.40
13	78	39	2.34	65	3.90	91	5.46
14	84	40	2.40	66	3.96	92	5.52
15	90	41	2.46	67	4.02	93	5.58
16	96	42	2.52	68	4.08	94	5.64
17	1.02	43	2.58	69	4.14	95	5.70
18	1.08	44	2.64	70	4.20	96	5.76
19	1.14	45	2.70	71	4.26	97	5.82
20	1.20	46	2.76	72	4.32	98	5.88
21	1.26	47	2.82	73	4.38	99	5.94
22	1.32	48	2.88	74	4.44	100	6.00
23	1.38	49	2.94	75	4.50	200	12.00
24	1.44	50	3.00	76	4.56	400	24.00
25	1.50	51	3.06	77	4.62	600	36.00
26	1.56	52	3.12	78	4.68	1000	60.00

6½ NEW PENCE

	£.np.		£.np.		£.np.		£.np.
1	6½	27	1.75½	53	3.44½	79	5.13½
2	13	28	1.82	54	3.51	80	5.20
3	19½	29	1.88½	55	3.57½	81	5.26½
4	26	30	1.95	56	3.64	82	5.33
5	32½	31	2.01½	57	3.70½	83	5.39½
6	39	32	2.08	58	3.77	84	5.46
7	45½	33	2.14½	59	3.83½	85	5.52½
8	52	34	2.21	60	3.90	86	5.59
9	58½	35	2.27½	61	3.96½	87	5.65½
10	65	36	2.34	62	4.03	88	5.72
11	71½	37	2.40½	63	4.09½	89	5.78½
12	78	38	2.47	64	4.16	90	5.85
13	84½	39	2.53½	65	4.22½	91	5.91½
14	91	40	2.60	66	4.29	92	5.98
15	97½	41	2.66½	67	4.35½	93	6.04½
16	1.04	42	2.73	68	4.42	94	6.11
17	1.10½	43	2.79½	69	4.48½	95	6.17½
18	1.17	44	2.86	70	4.55	96	6.24
19	1.23½	45	2.92½	71	4.61½	97	6.30½
20	1.30	46	2.99	72	4.68	98	6.37
21	1.36½	47	3.05½	73	4.74½	99	6.43½
22	1.43	48	3.12	74	4.81	100	6.50
23	1.49½	49	3.18½	75	4.87½	200	13.00
24	1.56	50	3.25	76	4.94	400	26.00
25	1.62½	51	3.31½	77	5.00½	600	39.00
26	1.69	52	3.38	78	5.07	1000	65.00

7 NEW PENCE

	£.np.		£.np		£.np.		£.np.
1	7	27	1.89	53	3.71	79	5.53
2	14	28	1.96	54	3.78	80	5.60
3	21	29	2.03	55	3.85	81	5.67
4	28	30	2.10	56	3.92	82	5.74
5	35	31	2.17	57	3.99	83	5.81
6	42	32	2.24	58	4.06	84	5.88
7	49	33	2.31	59	4.13	85	5.95
8	56	34	2.38	60	4.20	86	6.02
9	63	35	2.45	61	4.27	87	6.09
10	70	36	2.52	62	4.34	88	6.16
11	77	37	2.59	63	4.41	89	6.23
12	84	38	2.66	64	4.48	90	6.30
13	91	39	2.73	65	4.55	91	6.37
14	98	40	2.80	66	4.62	92	6.44
15	1.05	41	2.87	67	4.69	93	6.51
16	1.12	42	2.94	68	4.76	94	6.58
17	1.19	43	3.01	69	4.83	95	6.65
18	1.26	44	3.08	70	4.90	96	6.72
19	1.33	45	3.15	71	4.97	97	6.79
20	1.40	46	3.22	72	5.04	98	6.86
21	1.47	47	3.29	73	5.11	99	6.93
22	1.54	48	3.36	74	5.18	100	7.00
23	1.61	49	3.43	75	5.25	200	14.00
24	1.68	50	3.50	76	5.32	400	28.00
25	1.75	51	3.57	77	5.39	600	42.00
26	1.82	52	3.64	78	5.46	1000	70.00

	£.np.		£.np.		£.np.		£.np.
1	7½	27	2.02½	53	3.97½	79	5.92½
2	15	28	2.10	54	4.05	80	6.00
3	22½	29	2.17½	55	4.12½	81	6.07½
4	30	30	2.25	56	4.20	82	6.15
5	37½	31	2.32½	57	4.27½	83	6.22½
6	45	32	2.40	58	4.35	84	6.30
7	52½	33	2.47½	59	4.42½	85	6.37½
8	60	34	2.55	60	4.50	86	6.45
9	67½	35	2.62½	61	4.57½	87	6.52½
10	75	36	2.70	62	4.65	88	6.60
11	82½	37	2.77½	63	4.72½	89	6.67½
12	90	38	2.85	64	4.80	90	6.75
13	97½	39	2.92½	65	4.87½	91	6.82½
14	1.05	40	3.00	66	4.95	92	6.90
15	1.12½	41	3.07½	67	5.02½	93	6.97½
16	1.20	42	3.15	68	5.10	94	7.05
17	1.27½	43	3.22½	69	5.17½	95	7.12½
18	1.35	44	3.30	70	5.25	96	7.20
19	1.42½	45	3.37½	71	5.32½	97	7.27½
20	1.50	46	3.45	72	5.40	98	7.35
21	1.57½	47	3.52½	73	5.47½	99	7.42½
22	1.65	48	3.60	74	5.55	100	7.50
23	1.72½	49	3.67½	75	5.62½	200	15.00
24	1.80	50	3.75	76	5.70	400	30.00
25	1.87½	51	3.82½	77	5.77½	600	45.00
26	1.95	52	3.90	78	5.85	1000	75.00

8 NEW PENCE

	£.np.		£.np.		£.np.		£.np.
1	8	27	2.16	53	4.24	79	6.32
2	16	28	2.24	54	4.32	80	6.40
3	24	29	2.32	55	4.40	81	6.48
4	32	30	2.40	56	4.48	82	6.56
5	40	31	2.48	57	4.56	83	6.64
6	48	32	2.56	58	4.64	84	6.72
7	56	33	2.64	59	4.72	85	6.80
8	64	34	2.72	60	4.80	86	6.88
9	72	35	2.80	61	4.88	87	6.96
10	80	36	2.88	62	4.96	88	7.04
11	88	37	2.96	63	5.04	89	7.12
12	96	38	3.04	64	5.12	90	7.20
13	1.04	39	3.12	65	5.20	91	7.28
14	1.12	40	3.20	66	5.28	92	7.36
15	1.20	41	3.28	67	5.36	93	7.44
16	1.28	42	3.36	68	5.44	94	7.52
17	1.36	43	3.44	69	5.52	95	7.60
18	1.44	44	3.52	70	5.60	96	7.68
19	1.52	45	3.60	71	5.68	97	7.76
20	1.60	46	3.68	72	5.76	98	7.84
21	1.68	47	3.76	73	5.84	99	7.92
22	1.76	48	3.84	74	5.92	100	8.00
23	1.84	49	3.92	75	6.00	200	16.00
24	1.92	50	4.00	76	6.08	400	32.00
25	2.00	51	4.08	77	6.16	600	48.00
26	2.08	52	4.16	78	6.24	1000	80.00

	£.np.		£.np.		£.np.		£.np.
1	8½	27	2.29½	53	4.50½	79	6.71½
2	17	28	2.38	54	4.59	80	6.80
3	25½	29	2.46½	55	4.67½	81	6.88½
4	34	30	2.55	56	4.76	82	6.97
5	42½	31	2.63½	57	4.84½	83	7.05½
6	51	32	2.72	58	4.93	84	7.14
7	59½	33	2.80½	59	5.01½	85	7.22½
8	68	34	2.89	60	5.10	86	7.31
9	76½	35	2.97½	61	5.18½	87	7.39½
10	85	36	3.06	62	5.27	88	7.48
11	93½	37	3.14½	63	5.35½	89	7.56½
12	1.02	38	3.23	64	5.44	90	7.65
13	1.10½	39	3.31½	65	5.52½	91	7.73½
14	1.19	40	3.40	66	5.61	92	7.82
15	1.27½	41	3.48½	67	5.69½	93	7.90½
16	1.36	42	3.57	68	5.78	94	7.99
17	1.44½	43	3.65½	69	5.86½	95	8.07½
18	1.53	44	3.74	70	5.95	96	8.16
19	1.61½	45	3.82½	71	6.03½	97	8.24½
20	1.70	46	3.91	72	6.12	98	8.33
21	1.78½	47	3.99½	73	6.20½	99	8.41½
22	1.87	48	4.08	74	6.29	100	8.50
23	1.95½	49	4.16½	75	6.37½	200	17.00
24	2.04	50	4.25	76	6.46	400	34.00
25	2.12½	51	4.33½	77	6.54½	600	51.00
26	2.21	52	4.42	78	6.63	1000	85.00

	£.np.		£.np.		£.np.		£.np.
1	9	27	2.43	53	4.77	79	7.11
2	18	28	2.52	54	4.86	80	7.20
3	27	29	2.61	55	4.95	81	7.29
4	36	30	2.70	56	5.04	82	7.38
5	45	31	2.79	57	5.13	83	7.47
6	54	32	2.88	58	5.22	84	7.56
7	63	33	2.97	59	5.31	85	7.65
8	72	34	3.06	60	5.40	86	7.74
9	81	35	3.15	61	5.49	87	7.83
10	90	36	3.24	62	5.58	88	7.92
11	99	37	3.33	63	5.67	89	8.01
12	1.08	38	3.42	64	5.76	90	8.10
13	1.17	39	3.51	65	5.85	91	8.19
14	1.26	40	3.60	66	5.94	92	8.28
15	1.35	41	3.69	67	6.03	93	8.37
16	1.44	42	3.78	68	6.12	94	8.46
17	1.53	43	3.87	69	6.21	95	8.55
18	1.62	44	3.96	70	6.30	96	8.64
19	1.71	45	4.05	71	6.39	97	8.73
20	1.80	46	4.14	72	6.48	98	8.82
21	1.89	47	4.23	73	6.57	99	8.91
22	1.98	48	4.32	74	6.66	100	9.00
23	2.07	49	4.41	75	6.75	200	18.00
24	2.16	50	4.50	76	6.84	400	36.00
25	2.25	51	4.59	77	6.93	600	54.00
26	2.34	52	4.68	78	7.02	1000	90.00

	£.np.		£.np.		£.np.		£.np.
1	9½	27	2.56½	53	5.03½	79	7.50½
2	19	28	2.66	54	5.13	80	7.60
3	28½	29	2.75½	55	5.22½	81	7.69½
4	38	30	2.85	56	5.32	82	7.79
5	47½	31	2.94½	57	5.41½	83	7.88½
6	57	32	3.04	58	5.51	84	7.98
7	66½	33	3.13½	59	5.60½	85	8.07½
8	76	34	3.23	60	5.70	86	8.17
9	85½	35	3.32½	61	5.79½	87	8.26½
10	95	36	3.42	62	5.89	88	8.36
11	1.04½	37	3.51½	63	5.98½	89	8.45½
12	1.14	38	3.61	64	6.08	90	8.55
13	1.23½	39	3.70½	65	6.17½	91	8.64½
14	1.33	40	3.80	66	6.27	92	8.74
15	1.42½	41	3.89½	67	6.36½	93	8.83½
16	1.52	42	3.99	68	6.46	94	8.93
17	1.61½	43	4.08½	69	6.55½	95	9.02½
18	1.71	44	4.18	70	6.65	96	9.12
19	1.80½	45	4.27½	71	6.74½	97	9.21½
20	1.90	46	4.37	72	6.84	98	9.31
21	1.99½	47	4.46½	73	6.93½	99	9.40½
22	2.09	48	4.56	74	7.03	100	9.50
23	2.18½	49	4.65½	75	7.12½	200	19.00
24	2.28	50	4.75	76	7.22	400	38.00
25	2.37½	51	4.84½	77	7.31½	600	57.00
26	2.47	52	4.94	78	7.41	1000	95.00

10 NEW PENCE

	£.np.		£.np.		£.np.		£.np.
1	10	27	2.70	53	5.30	79	7.90
2	20	28	2.80	54	5.40	80	8.00
3	30	29	2.90	55	5.50	81	8.10
4	40	30	3.00	56	5.60	82	8.20
5	50	31	3.10	57	5.70	83	8.30
6	60	32	3.20	58	5.80	84	8.40
7	70	33	3.30	59	5.90	85	8.50
8	80	34	3.40	60	6.00	86	8.60
9	90	35	3.50	61	6.10	87	8.70
10	1.00	36	3.60	62	6.20	88	8.80
11	1.10	37	3.70	63	6.30	89	8.90
12	1.20	38	3.80	64	6.40	90	9.00
13	1.30	39	3.90	65	6.50	91	9.10
14	1.40	40	4.00	66	6.60	92	9.20
15	1.50	41	4.10	67	6.70	93	9.30
16	1.60	42	4.20	68	6.80	94	9.40
17	1.70	43	4.30	69	6.90	95	9.50
18	1.80	44	4.40	70	7.00	96	9.60
19	1.90	45	4.50	71	7.10	97	9.70
20	2.00	46	4.60	72	7.20	98	9.80
21	2.10	47	4.70	73	7.30	99	9.90
22	2.20	48	4.80	74	7.40	100	10.00
23	2.30	49	4.90	75	7.50	200	20.00
24	2.40	50	5.00	76	7.60	400	40.00
25	2.50	51	5.10	77	7.70	600	60.00
26	2.60	52	5.20	78	7.80	1000	100.00

10½ NEW PENCE

	£.np.		£.np.		£.np.		£.np.
1	10½	27	2.83½	53	5.56½	79	8.29½
2	21	28	2.94	54	5.67	80	8.40
3	31½	29	3.04½	55	5.77½	81	8.50½
4	42	30	3.15	56	5.88	82	8.61
5	52½	31	3.25½	57	5.98½	83	8.71½
6	63	32	3.36	58	6.09	84	8.82
7	73½	33	3.46½	59	6.19½	85	8.92½
8	84	34	3.57	60	6.30	86	9.03
9	94½	35	3.67½	61	6.40½	87	9.13½
10	1.05	36	3.78	62	6.51	88	9.24
11	1.15½	37	3.88½	63	6.61½	89	9.34½
12	1.26	38	3.99	64	6.72	90	9.45
13	1.36½	39	4.09½	65	6.82½	91	9.55½
14	1.47	40	4.20	66	6.93	92	9.66
15	1.57½	41	4.30½	67	7.03½	93	9.76½
16	1.68	42	4.41	68	7.14	94	9.87
17	1.78½	43	4.51½	69	7.24½	95	9.97½
18	1.89	44	4.62	70	7.35	96	10.08
19	1.99½	45	4.72½	71	7.45½	97	10.18½
20	2.10	46	4.83	72	7.56	98	10.29
21	2.20½	47	4.93½	73	7.66½	99	10.39½
22	2.31	48	5.04	74	7.77	100	10.50
23	2.41½	49	5.14½	75	7.87½	200	21.00
24	2.52	50	5.25	76	7.98	400	42.00
25	2.62½	51	5.35½	77	8.08½	600	63.00
26	2.73	52	5.46	78	8.19	1000	105.00

11 NEW PENCE

	£.np.		£.np.		£.np.		£.np.
1	11	27	2.97	53	5.83	79	8.69
2	22	28	3.08	54	5.94	80	8.80
3	33	29	3.19	55	6.05	81	8.91
4	44	30	3.30	56	6.16	82	9.02
5	55	31	3.41	57	6.27	83	9.13
6	66	32	3.52	58	6.38	84	9.24
7	77	33	3.63	59	6.49	85	9.35
8	88	34	3.74	60	6.60	86	9.46
9	99	35	3.85	61	6.71	87	9.57
10	1.10	36	3.96	62	6.82	88	9.68
11	1.21	37	4.07	63	6.93	89	9.79
12	1.32	38	4.18	64	7.04	90	9.90
13	1.43	39	4.29	65	7.15	91	10.01
14	1.54	40	4.40	66	7.26	92	10.12
15	1.65	41	4.51	67	7.37	93	10.23
16	1.76	42	4.62	68	7.48	94	10.34
17	1.87	43	4.73	69	7.59	95	10.45
18	1.98	44	4.84	70	7.70	96	10.56
19	2.09	45	4.95	71	7.81	97	10.67
20	2.20	46	5.06	72	7.92	98	10.78
21	2.31	47	5.17	73	8.03	99	10.89
22	2.42	48	5.28	74	8.14	100	11.00
23	2.53	49	5.39	75	8.25	200	22.00
24	2.64	50	5.50	76	8.36	400	44.00
25	2.75	51	5.61	77	8.47	600	66.00
26	2.86	52	5.72	78	8.58	1000	110.00

	£.np.		£.np.		£.np.		£.np.
1	11½	27	3.10½	53	6.09½	79	9.08½
2	23	28	3.22	54	6.21	80	9.20
3	34½	29	3.33½	55	6.32½	81	9.31½
4	46	30	3.45	56	6.44	82	9.43
5	57½	31	3.56½	57	6.55½	83	9.54½
6	69	32	3.68	58	6.67	84	9.66
7	80½	33	3.79½	59	6.78½	85	9.77½
8	92	34	3.91	60	6.90	86	9.89
9	1.03½	35	4.02½	61	7.01½	87	10.00½
10	1.15	36	4.14	62	7.13	88	10.12
11	1.26½	37	4.25½	63	7.24½	89	10.23½
12	1.38	38	4.37	64	7.36	90	10.35
13	1.49½	39	4.48½	65	7.47½	91	10.46½
14	1.61	40	4.60	66	7.59	92	10.58
15	1.72½	41	4.71½	67	7.70½	93	10.69½
16	1.84	42	4.83	68	7.82	94	10.81
17	1.95½	43	4.94½	69	7.93½	95	10.92½
18	2.07	44	5.06	70	8.05	96	11.04
19	2.18½	45	5.17½	71	8.16½	97	11.15½
20	2.30	46	5.29	72	8.28	98	11.27
21	2.41½	47	5.40½	73	8.39½	99	11.38½
22	2.53	48	5.52	74	8.51	100	11.50
23	2.64½	49	5.63½	75	8.62½	200	23.00
24	2.76	50	5.75	76	8.74	400	46.00
25	2.87½	51	5.86½	77	8.85½	600	69.00
26	2.99	52	5.98	78	8.97	1000	115.00

	£.np.		£.np.		£.np.		£.np.
1	12	27	3.24	53	6.36	79	9.48
2	24	28	3.36	54	6.48	80	9.60
3	36	29	3.48	55	6.60	81	9.72
4	48	30	3.60	56	6.72	82	9.84
5	60	31	3.72	57	6.84	83	9.96
6	72	32	3.84	58	6.96	84	10.08
7	84	33	3.96	59	7.08	85	10.20
8	96	34	4.08	60	7.20	86	10.32
9	1.08	35	4.20	61	7.32	87	10.44
10	1.20	36	4.32	62	7.44	88	10.56
11	1.32	37	4.44	63	7.56	89	10.68
12	1.44	38	4.56	64	7.68	90	10.80
13	1.56	39	4.68	65	7.80	91	10.92
14	1.68	40	4.80	66	7.92	92	11.04
15	1.80	41	4.92	67	8.04	93	11.16
16	1.92	42	5.04	68	8.16	94	11.28
17	2.04	43	5.16	69	8.28	95	11.40
18	2.16	44	5.28	70	8.40	96	11.52
19	2.28	45	5.40	71	8.52	97	11.64
20	2.40	46	5.52	72	8.64	98	11.76
21	2.52	47	5.64	73	8.76	99	11.88
22	2.64	48	5.76	74	8.88	100	12.00
23	2.76	49	5.88	75	9.00	200	24.00
24	2.88	50	6.00	76	9.12	400	48.00
25	3.00	51	6.12	77	9.24	600	72.00
26	3.12	52	6.24	78	9.36	1000	120.00

	£.np.		£.np.		£.np.		£.np.
1	12½	27	3.37½	53	6.62½	79	9.87½
2	25	28	3.50	54	6.75	80	10.00
3	37½	29	3.62½	55	6.87½	81	10.12½
4	50	30	3.75	56	7.00	82	10.25
5	62½	31	3.87½	57	7.12½	83	10.37½
6	75	32	4.00	58	7.25	84	10.50
7	87½	33	4.12½	59	7.37½	85	10.62½
8	1.00	34	4.25	60	7.50	86	10.75
9	1.12½	35	4.37½	61	7.62½	87	10.87½
10	1.25	36	4.50	62	7.75	88	11.00
11	1.37½	37	4.62½	63	7.87½	89	11.12½
12	1.50	38	4.75	64	8.00	90	11.25
13	1.62½	39	4.87½	65	8.12½	91	11.37½
14	1.75	40	5.00	66	8.25	92	11.50
15	1.87½	41	5.12½	67	8.37½	93	11.62½
16	2.00	42	5.25	68	8.50	94	11.75
17	2.12½	43	5.37½	69	8.62½	95	11.87½
18	2.25	44	5.50	70	8.75	96	12.00
19	2.37½	45	5.62½	71	8.87½	97	12.12½
20	2.50	46	5.75	72	9.00	98	12.25
21	2.62½	47	5.87½	73	9.12½	99	12.37½
22	2.75	48	6.00	74	9.25	100	12.50
23	2.87½	49	6.12½	75	9.37½	200	25.00
24	3.00	50	6.25	76	9.50	400	50.00
25	3.12½	51	6.37½	77	9.62½	600	75.00
26	3.25	52	6.50	78	9.75	1000	125.00

	£.np.		£.np.		£.np.		£.np.
1	13	27	3.51	53	6.89	79	10.27
2	26	28	3.64	54	7.02	80	10.40
3	39	29	3.77	55	7.15	81	10.53
4	52	30	3.90	56	7.28	82	10.66
5	65	31	4.03	57	7.41	83	10.79
6	78	32	4.16	58	7.54	84	10.92
7	91	33	4.29	59	7.67	85	11.05
8	1.04	34	4.42	60	7.80	86	11.18
9	1.17	35	4.55	61	7.93	87	11.31
10	1.30	36	4.68	62	8.06	88	11.44
11	1.43	37	4.81	63	8.19	89	11.57
12	1.56	38	4.94	64	8.32	90	11.70
13	1.69	39	5.07	65	8.45	91	11.83
14	1.82	40	5.20	66	8.58	92	11.96
15	1.95	41	5.33	67	8.71	93	12.09
16	2.08	42	5.46	68	8.84	94	12.22
17	2.21	43	5.59	69	8.97	95	12.35
18	2.34	44	5.72	70	9.10	96	12.48
19	2.47	45	5.85	71	9.23	97	12.61
20	2.60	46	5.98	72	9.36	98	12.74
21	2.73	47	6.11	73	9.49	99	12.87
22	2.86	48	6.24	74	9.62	100	13.00
23	2.99	49	6.37	75	9.75	200	26.00
24	3.12	50	6.50	76	9.88	400	52.00
25	3.25	51	6.63	77	10.01	600	78.00
26	3.38	52	6.76	78	10.14	1000	130.00

	£.np.		£.np.		£.np.		£.np.
1	13½	27	3.64½	53	7.15½	79	10.66½
2	27	28	3.78	54	7.29	80	10.80
3	40½	29	3.91½	55	7.42½	81	10.93½
4	54	30	4.05	56	7.56	82	11.07
5	67½	31	4.18½	57	7.69½	83	11.20½
6	81	32	4.32	58	7.83	84	11.34
7	94½	33	4.45½	59	7.96½	85	11.47½
8	1.08	34	4.59	60	8.10	86	11.61
9	1.21½	35	4.72½	61	8.23½	87	11.74½
10	1.35	36	4.86	62	8.37	88	11.88
11	1.48½	37	4.99½	63	8.50½	89	12.01½
12	1.62	38	5.13	64	8.64	90	12.15
13	1.75½	39	5.26½	65	8.77½	91	12.28½
14	1.89	40	5.40	66	8.91	92	12.42
15	2.02½	41	5.53½	67	9.04½	93	12.55½
16	2.16	42	5.67	68	9.18	94	12.69
17	2.29½	43	5.80½	69	9.31½	95	12.82½
18	2.43	44	5.94	70	9.45	96	12.96
19	2.56½	45	6.07½	71	9.58½	97	13.09½
20	2.70	46	6.21	72	9.72	98	13.23
21	2.83½	47	6.34½	73	9.85½	99	13.36½
22	2.97	48	6.48	74	9.99	100	13.50
23	3.10½	49	6.61½	75	10.12½	200	27.00
24	3.24	50	6.75	76	10.26	400	54.00
25	3.37½	51	6.88½	77	10.39½	600	81.00
26	3.51	52	7.02	78	10.53	1000	135.00

14 NEW PENCE

	£.np.		£.np.		£.np.		£.np.
1	14	27	3.78	53	7.42	79	11.06
2	28	28	3.92	54	7.56	80	11.20
3	42	29	4.06	55	7.70	81	11.34
4	56	30	4.20	56	7.84	82	11.48
5	70	31	4.34	57	7.98	83	11.62
6	84	32	4.48	58	8.12	84	11.76
7	98	33	4.62	59	8.26	85	11.90
8	1.12	34	4.76	60	8.40	86	12.04
9	1.26	35	4.90	61	8.54	87	12.18
10	1.40	36	5.04	62	8.68	88	12.32
11	1.54	37	5.18	63	8.82	89	12.46
12	1.68	38	5.32	64	8.96	90	12.60
13	1.82	39	5.46	65	9.10	91	12.74
14	1.96	40	5.60	66	9.24	92	12.88
15	2.10	41	5.74	67	9.38	93	13.02
16	2.24	42	5.88	68	9.52	94	13.16
17	2.38	43	6.02	69	9.66	95	13.30
18	2.52	44	6.16	70	9.80	96	13.44
19	2.66	45	6.30	71	9.94	97	13.58
20	2.80	46	6.44	72	10.08	98	13.72
21	2.94	47	6.58	73	10.22	99	13.86
22	3.08	48	6.72	74	10.36	100	14.00
23	3.22	49	6.86	75	10.50	200	28.00
24	3.36	50	7.00	76	10.64	400	56.00
25	3.50	51	7.14	77	10.78	600	84.00
26	3.64	52	7.28	78	10.92	1000	140.00

	£.np.		£.np.		£.np.		£.np.
1	14½	27	3.91½	53	7.68½	79	11.45½
2	29	28	4.06	54	7.83	80	11.60
3	43½	29	4.20½	55	7.97½	81	11.74½
4	58	30	4.35	56	8.12	82	11.89
5	72½	31	4.49½	57	8.26½	83	12.03½
6	87	32	4.64	58	8.41	84	12.18
7	1.01½	33	4.78½	59	8.55½	85	12.32½
8	1.16	34	4.93	60	8.70	86	12.47
9	1.30½	35	5.07½	61	8.84½	87	12.61½
10	1.45	36	5.22	62	8.99	88	12.76
11	1.59½	37	5.36½	63	9.13½	89	12.90½
12	1.74	38	5.51	64	9.28	90	13.05
13	1.88½	39	5.65½	65	9.42½	91	13.19½
14	2.03	40	5.80	66	9.57	92	13.34
15	2.17½	41	5.94½	67	9.71½	93	13.48½
16	2.32	42	6.09	68	9.86	94	13.63
17	2.46½	43	6.23½	69	10.00½	95	13.77½
18	2.61	44	6.38	70	10.15	96	13.92
19	2.75½	45	6.52½	71	10.29½	97	14.06½
20	2.90	46	6.67	72	10.44	98	14.21
21	3.04½	47	6.81½	73	10.58½	99	14.35½
22	3.19	48	6.96	74	10.73	100	14.50
23	3.33½	49	7.10½	75	10.87½	200	29.00
24	3.48	50	7.25	76	11.02	400	58.00
25	3.62½	51	7.39½	77	11.16½	600	87.00
26	3.77	52	7.54	78	11.31	1000	145.00

	£.np.		£.np.		£.np.		£.np.
1	15	27	4.05	53	7.95	79	11.85
2	30	28	4.20	54	8.10	80	12.00
3	45	29	4.35	55	8.25	81	12.15
4	60	30	4.50	56	8.40	82	12.30
5	75	31	4.65	57	8.55	83	12.45
6	90	32	4.80	58	8.70	84	12.60
7	1.05	33	4.95	59	8.85	85	12.75
8	1.20	34	5.10	60	9.00	86	12.90
9	1.35	35	5.25	61	9.15	87	13.05
10	1.50	36	5.40	62	9.30	88	13.20
11	1.65	37	5.55	63	9.45	89	13.35
12	1.80	38	5.70	64	9.60	90	13.50
13	1.95	39	5.85	65	9.75	91	13.65
14	2.10	40	6.00	66	9.90	92	13.80
15	2.25	41	6.15	67	10.05	93	13.95
16	2.40	42	6.30	68	10.20	94	14.10
17	2.55	43	6.45	69	10.35	95	14.25
18	2.70	44	6.60	70	10.50	96	14.40
19	2.85	45	6.75	71	10.65	97	14.55
20	3.00	46	6.90	72	10.80	98	14.70
21	3.15	47	7.05	73	10.95	99	14.85
22	3.30	48	7.20	74	11.10	100	15.00
23	3.45	49	7.35	75	11.25	200	30.00
24	3.60	50	7.50	76	11.40	400	60.00
25	3.75	51	7.65	77	11.55	600	90.00
26	3.90	52	7.80	78	11.70	1000	150.00

3

15½ NEW PENCE

	£.np.		£.np.		£.np.		£.np.
1	15½	27	4.18½	53	8.21½	79	12.24½
2	31	28	4.34	54	8.37	80	12.40
3	46½	29	4.49½	55	8.52½	81	12.55½
4	62	30	4.65	56	8.68	82	12.71
5	77½	31	4.80½	57	8.83½	83	12.86½
6	93	32	4.96	58	8.99	84	13.02
7	1.08½	33	5.11½	59	9.14½	85	13.17½
8	1.24	34	5.27	60	9.30	86	13.33
9	1.39½	35	5.42½	61	9.45½	87	13.48½
10	1.55	36	5.58	62	9.61	88	13.64
11	1.70½	37	5.73½	63	9.76½	89	13.79½
12	1.86	38	5.89	64	9.92	90	13.95
13	2.01½	39	6.04½	65	10.07½	91	14.10½
14	2.17	40	6.20	66	10.23	92	14.26
15	2.32½	41	6.35½	67	10.38½	93	14.41½
16	2.48	42	6.51	68	10.54	94	14.57
17	2.63½	43	6.66½	69	10.69½	95	14.72½
18	2.79	44	6.82	70	10.85	96	14.88
19	2.94½	45	6.97½	71	11.00½	97	15.03½
20	3.10	46	7.13	72	11.16	98	15.19
21	3.25½	47	7.28½	73	11.31½	99	15.34½
22	3.41	48	7.44	74	11.47	100	15.50
23	3.56½	49	7.59½	75	11.62½	200	31.00
24	3.72	50	7.75	76	11.78	400	62.00
25	3.87½	51	7.90½	77	11.93½	600	93.00
26	4.03	52	8.06	78	12.09	1000	155.00

	£.np.		£.np.		£.np.		£.np.
1	16	27	4.32	53	8.48	79	12.64
2	32	28	4.48	54	8.64	80	12.80
3	48	29	4.64	55	8.80	81	12.96
4	64	30	4.80	56	8.96	82	13.12
5	80	31	4.96	57	9.12	83	13.28
6	96	32	5.12	58	9.28	84	13.44
7	1.12	33	5.28	59	9.44	85	13.60
8	1.28	34	5.44	60	9.60	86	13.76
9	1.44	35	5.60	61	9.76	87	13.92
10	1.60	36	5.76	62	9.92	88	14.08
11	1.76	37	5.92	63	10.08	89	14.24
12	1.92	38	6.08	64	10.24	90	14.40
13	2.08	39	6.24	65	10.40	91	14.56
14	2.24	40	6.40	66	10.56	92	14.72
15	2.40	41	6.56	67	10.72	93	14.88
16	2.56	42	6.72	68	10.88	94	15.04
17	2.72	43	6.88	69	11.04	95	15.20
18	2.88	44	7.04	70	11.20	96	15.36
19	3.04	45	7.20	71	11.36	97	15.52
20	3.20	46	7.36	72	11.52	98	15.68
21	3.36	47	7.52	73	11.68	99	15.84
22	3.52	48	7.68	74	11.84	100	16.00
23	3.68	49	7.84	75	12.00	200	32.00
24	3.84	50	8.00	76	12.16	400	64.00
25	4.00	51	8.16	77	12.32	600	96.00
26	4.16	52	8.32	78	12.48	1000	160.00

	£.np.		£.np.		£.np.		£.np.
1	16½	27	4.45½	53	8.74½	79	13.03½
2	33	28	4.62	54	8.91	80	13.20
3	49½	29	4.78½	55	9.07½	81	13.36½
4	66	30	4.95	56	9.24	82	13.53
5	82½	31	5.11½	57	9.40½	83	13.69½
6	99	32	5.28	58	9.57	84	13.86
7	1.15½	33	5.44½	59	9.73½	85	14.02½
8	1.32	34	5.61	60	9.90	86	14.19
9	1.48½	35	5.77½	61	10.06½	87	14.35½
10	1.65	36	5.94	62	10.23	88	14.52
11	1.81½	37	6.10½	63	10.39½	89	14.68½
12	1.98	38	6.27	64	10.56	90	14.85
13	2.14½	39	6.43½	65	10.72½	91	15.01½
14	2.31	40	6.60	66	10.89	92	15.18
15	2.47½	41	6.76½	67	11.05½	93	15.34½
16	2.64	42	6.93	68	11.22	94	15.51
17	2.80½	43	7.09½	69	11.38½	95	15.67½
18	2.97	44	7.26	70	11.55	96	15.84
19	3.13½	45	7.42½	71	11.71½	97	16.00½
20	3.30	46	7.59	72	11.88	98	16.17
21	3.46½	47	7.75½	73	12.04½	99	16.33½
22	3.63	48	7.92	74	12.21	100	16.50
23	3.79½	49	8.08½	75	12.37½	200	33.00
24	3.96	50	8.25	76	12.54	400	66.00
25	4.12½	51	8.41½	77	12.70½	600	99.00
26	4.29	52	8.58	78	12.87	1000	165.00

	£.np.		£.np.		£.np.		£.np.
1	17	27	4.59	53	9.01	79	13.43
2	34	28	4.76	54	9.18	80	13.60
3	51	29	4.93	55	9.35	81	13.77
4	68	30	5.10	56	9.52	82	13.94
5	85	31	5.27	57	9.69	83	14.11
6	1.02	32	5.44	58	9.86	84	14.28
7	1.19	33	5.61	59	10.03	85	14.45
8	1.36	34	5.78	60	10.20	86	14.62
9	1.53	35	5.95	61	10.37	87	14.79
10	1.70	36	6.12	62	10.54	88	14.96
11	1.87	37	6.29	63	10.71	89	15.13
12	2.04	38	6.46	64	10.88	90	15.30
13	2.21	39	6.63	65	11.05	91	15.47
14	2.38	40	6.80	66	11.22	92	15.64
15	2.55	41	6.97	67	11.39	93	15.81
16	2.72	42	7.14	68	11.56	94	15.98
17	2.89	43	7.31	69	11.73	95	16.15
18	3.06	44	7.48	70	11.90	96	16.32
19	3.23	45	7.65	71	12.07	97	16.49
20	3.40	46	7.82	72	12.24	98	16.66
21	3.57	47	7.99	73	12.41	99	16.83
22	3.74	48	8.16	74	12.58	100	17.00
23	3.91	49	8.33	75	12.75	200	34.00
24	4.08	50	8.50	76	12.92	400	68.00
25	4.25	51	8.67	77	13.09	600	102.00
26	4.42	52	8.84	78	13.26	1000	170.00

17½ NEW PENCE

	£.np.		£.np.		£.np.		£.np.
1	17½	27	4.72½	53	9.27½	79	13.82½
2	35	28	4.90	54	9.45	80	14.00
3	52½	29	5.07½	55	9.62½	81	14.17½
4	70	30	5.25	56	9.80	82	14.35
5	87½	31	5.42½	57	9.97½	83	14.52½
6	1.05	32	5.60	58	10.15	84	14.70
7	1.22½	33	5.77½	59	10.32½	85	14.87½
8	1.40	34	5.95	60	10.50	86	15.05
9	1.57½	35	6.12½	61	10.67½	87	15.22½
10	1.75	36	6.30	62	10.85	88	15.40
11	1.92½	37	6.47½	63	11.02½	89	15.57½
12	2.10	38	6.65	64	11.20	90	15.75
13	2.27½	39	6.82½	65	11.37½	91	15.92½
14	2.45	40	7.00	66	11.55	92	16.10
15	2.62½	41	7.17½	67	11.72½	93	16.27½
16	2.80	42	7.35	68	11.90	94	16.45
17	2.97½	43	7.52½	69	12.07½	95	16.62½
18	3.15	44	7.70	70	12.25	96	16.80
19	3.32½	45	7.87½	71	12.42½	97	16.97½
20	3.50	46	8.05	72	12.60	98	17.15
21	3.67½	47	8.22½	73	12.77½	99	17.32½
22	3.85	48	8.40	74	12.95	100	17.50
23	4.02½	49	8.57½	75	13.12½	200	35.00
24	4.20	50	8.75	76	13.30	400	70.00
25	4.37½	51	8.92½	77	13.47½	600	105.00
26	4.55	52	9.10	78	13.65	1000	175.00

	£.np.		£.np.		£.np.		£.np.
1	18	27	4.86	53	9.54	79	14.22
2	36	28	5.04	54	9.72	80	14.40
3	54	29	5.22	55	9.90	81	14.58
4	72	30	5.40	56	10.08	82	14.76
5	90	31	5.58	57	10.26	83	14.94
6	1.08	32	5.76	58	10.44	84	15.12
7	1.26	33	5.94	59	10.62	85	15.30
8	1.44	34	6.12	60	10.80	86	15.48
9	1.62	35	6.30	61	10.98	87	15.66
10	1.80	36	6.48	62	11.16	88	15.84
11	1.98	37	6.66	63	11.34	89	16.02
12	2.16	38	6.84	64	11.52	90	16.20
13	2.34	39	7.02	65	11.70	91	16.38
14	2.52	40	7.20	66	11.88	92	16.56
15	2.70	41	7.38	67	12.06	93	16.74
16	2.88	42	7.56	68	12.24	94	16.92
17	3.06	43	7.74	69	12.42	95	17.10
18	3.24	44	7.92	70	12.60	96	17.28
19	3.42	45	8.10	71	12.78	97	17.46
20	3.60	46	8.28	72	12.96	98	17.64
21	3.78	47	8.46	73	13.14	99	17.82
22	3.96	48	8.64	74	13.32	100	18.00
23	4.14	49	8.82	75	13.50	200	36.00
24	4.32	50	9.00	76	13.68	400	72.00
25	4.50	51	9.18	77	13.86	600	108.00
26	4.68	52	9.36	78	14.04	1000	180.00

	£.np.		£.np.		£.np.		£.np.
1	18½	27	4.99½	53	9.80½	79	14.61½
2	37	28	5.18	54	9.99	80	14.80
3	55½	29	5.36½	55	10.17½	81	14.98½
4	74	30	5.55	56	10.36	82	15.17
5	92½	31	5.73½	57	10.54½	83	15.35½
6	1.11	32	5.92	58	10.73	84	15.54
7	1.29½	33	6.10½	59	10.91½	85	15.72½
8	1.48	34	6.29	60	11.10	86	15.91
9	1.66½	35	6.47½	61	11.28½	87	16.09½
10	1.85	36	6.66	62	11.47	88	16.28
11	2.03½	37	6.84½	63	11.65½	89	16.46½
12	2.22	38	7.03	64	11.84	90	16.65
13	2.40½	39	7.21½	65	12.02½	91	16.83½
14	2.59	40	7.40	66	12.21	92	17.02
15	2.77½	41	7.58½	67	12.39½	93	17.20½
16	2.96	42	7.77	68	12.58	94	17.39
17	3.14½	43	7.95½	69	12.76½	95	17.57½
18	3.33	44	8.14	70	12.95	96	17.76
19	3.51½	45	8.32½	71	13.13½	97	17.94½
20	3.70	46	8.51	72	13.32	98	18.13
21	3.88½	47	8.69½	73	13.50½	99	18.31½
22	4.07	48	8.88	74	13.69	100	18.50
23	4.25½	49	9.06½	75	13.87½	200	37.00
24	4.44	50	9.25	76	14.06	400	74.00
25	4.62½	51	9.43½	77	14.24½	600	111.00
26	4.81	52	9.62	78	14.43	1000	185.000

	£.np.		£.np.		£.np.		£.np.
1	19	27	5.13	53	10.07	79	15.01
2	38	28	5.32	54	10.26	80	15.20
3	57	29	5.51	55	10.45	81	15.39
4	76	30	5.70	56	10.64	82	15.58
5	95	31	5.89	57	10.83	83	15.77
6	1.14	32	6.08	58	11.02	84	15.96
7	1.33	33	6.27	59	11.21	85	16.15
8	1.52	34	6.46	60	11.40	86	16.34
9	1.71	35	6.65	61	11.59	87	16.53
10	1.90	36	6.84	62	11.78	88	16.72
11	2.09	37	7.03	63	11.97	89	16.91
12	2.28	38	7.22	64	12.16	90	17.10
13	2.47	39	7.41	65	12.35	91	17.29
14	2.66	40	7.60	66	12.54	92	17.48
15	2.85	41	7.79	67	12.73	93	17.67
16	3.04	42	7.98	68	12.92	94	17.86
17	3.23	43	8.17	69	13.11	95	18.05
18	3.42	44	8.36	70	13.30	96	18.24
19	3.61	45	8.55	71	13.49	97	18.43
20	3.80	46	8.74	72	13.68	98	18.62
21	3.99	47	8.93	73	13.87	99	18.81
22	4.18	48	9.12	74	14.06	100	19.00
23	4.37	49	9.31	75	14.25	200	38.00
24	4.56	50	9.50	76	14.44	400	76.00
25	4.75	51	9.69	77	14.63	600	114.00
26	4.94	52	9.88	78	14.82	1000	190.00

19½ NEW PENCE

	£.np.		£.np.		£.np.		£.np.
1	19½	27	5.26½	53	10.33½	79	15.40½
2	39	28	5.46	54	10.53	80	15.60
3	58½	29	5.65½	55	10.72½	81	15.79½
4	78	30	5.85	56	10.92	82	15.99
5	97½	31	6.04½	57	11.11½	83	16.18½
6	1.17	32	6.24	58	11.31	84	16.38
7	1.36½	33	6.43½	59	11.50½	85	16.57½
8	1.56	34	6.63	60	11.70	86	16.77
9	1.75½	35	6.82½	61	11.89½	87	16.96½
10	1.95	36	7.02	62	12.09	88	17.16
11	2.14½	37	7.21½	63	12.28½	89	17.35½
12	2.34	38	7.41	64	12.48	90	17.55
13	2.53½	39	7.60½	65	12.67½	91	17.74½
14	2.73	40	7.80	66	12.87	92	17.94
15	2.92½	41	7.99½	67	13.06½	93	18.13½
16	3.12	42	8.19	68	13.26	94	18.33
17	3.31½	43	8.38½	69	13.45½	95	18.52½
18	3.51	44	8.58	70	13.65	96	18.72
19	3.70½	45	8.77½	71	13.84½	97	18.91½
20	3.90	46	8.97	72	14.04	98	19.11
21	4.09½	47	9.16½	73	14.23½	99	19.30½
22	4.29	48	9.36	74	14.43	100	19.50
23	4.48½	49	9.55½	75	14.62½	200	39.00
24	4.68	50	9.75	76	14.82	400	78.00
25	4.87½	51	9.94½	77	15.01½	600	117.00
26	5.07	52	10.14	78	15.21	1000	195.00

	£.np.		£.np.		£.np.		£.np.
1	20	27	5.40	53	10.60	79	15.80
2	40	28	5.60	54	10.80	80	16.00
3	60	29	5.80	55	11.00	81	16.20
4	80	30	6.00	56	11.20	82	16.40
5	1.00	31	6.20	57	11.40	83	16.60
6	1.20	32	6.40	58	11.60	84	16.80
7	1.40	33	6.60	59	11.80	85	17.00
8	1.60	34	6.80	60	12.00	86	17.20
9	1.80	35	7.00	61	12.20	87	17.40
10	2.00	36	7.20	62	12.40	88	17.60
11	2.20	37	7.40	63	12.60	89	17.80
12	2.40	38	7.60	64	12.80	90	18.00
13	2.60	39	7.80	65	13.00	91	18.20
14	2.80	40	8.00	66	13.20	92	18.40
15	3.00	41	8.20	67	13.40	93	18.60
16	3.20	42	8.40	68	13.60	94	18.80
17	3.40	43	8.60	69	13.80	95	19.00
18	3.60	44	8.80	70	14.00	96	19.20
19	3.80	45	9.00	71	14.20	97	19.40
20	4.00	46	9.20	72	14.40	98	19.60
21	4.20	47	9.40	73	14.60	99	19.80
22	4.40	48	9.60	74	14.80	100	20.00
23	4.60	49	9.80	75	15.00	200	40.00
24	4.80	50	10.00	76	15.20	400	80.00
25	5.00	51	10.20	77	15.40	600	120.00
26	5.20	52	10.40	78	15.60	1000	200.00

	£.np.		£.np.		£.np.		£.np.
1	20½	27	5.53½	53	10.86½	79	16.19½
2	41	28	5.74	54	11.07	80	16.40
3	61½	29	5.94½	55	11.27½	81	16.60½
4	82	30	6.15	56	11.48	82	16.81
5	1.02½	31	6.35½	57	11.68½	83	17.01½
6	1.23	32	6.56	58	11.89	84	17.22
7	1.43½	33	6.76½	59	12.09½	85	17.42½
8	1.64	34	6.97	60	12.30	86	17.63
9	1.84½	35	7.17½	61	12.50½	87	17.83½
10	2.05	36	7.38	62	12.71	88	18.04
11	2.25½	37	7.58½	63	12.91½	89	18.24½
12	2.46	38	7.79	64	13.12	90	18.45
13	2.66½	39	7.99½	65	13.32½	91	18.65½
14	2.87	40	8.20	66	13.53	92	18.86
15	3.07½	41	8.40½	67	13.73½	93	19.06½
16	3.28	42	8.61	68	13.94	94	19.27
17	3.48½	43	8.81½	69	14.14½	95	19.47½
18	3.69	44	9.02	70	14.35	96	19.68
19	3.89½	45	9.22½	71	14.55½	97	19.88½
20	4.10	46	9.43	72	14.76	98	20.09
21	4.30½	47	9.63½	73	14.96½	99	20.29½
22	4.51	48	9.84	74	15.17	100	20.50
23	4.71½	49	10.04½	75	15.37½	200	41.00
24	4.92	50	10.25	76	15.58	400	82.00
25	5.12½	51	10.45½	77	15.78½	600	123.00
26	5.33	52	10.66	78	15.99	1000	205.00

21 NEW PENCE

	£.np.		£.np.		£.np.		£.np.
1	21	27	5.67	53	11.13	79	16.59
2	42	28	5.88	54	11.34	80	16.80
3	63	29	6.09	55	11.55	81	17.01
4	84	30	6.30	56	11.76	82	17.22
5	1.05	31	6.51	57	11.97	83	17.43
6	1.26	32	6.72	58	12.18	84	17.64
7	1.47	33	6.93	59	12.39	85	17.85
8	1.68	34	7.14	60	12.60	86	18.06
9	1.89	35	7.35	61	12.81	87	18.27
10	2.10	36	7.56	62	13.02	88	18.48
11	2.31	37	7.77	63	13.23	89	18.69
12	2.52	38	7.98	64	13.44	90	18.90
13	2.73	39	8.19	65	13.65	91	19.11
14	2.94	40	8.40	66	13.86	92	19.32
15	3.15	41	8.61	67	14.07	93	19.53
16	3.36	42	8.82	68	14.28	94	19.74
17	3.57	43	9.03	69	14.49	95	19.95
18	3.78	44	9.24	70	14.70	96	20.16
19	3.99	45	9.45	71	14.91	97	20.37
20	4.20	46	9.66	72	15.12	98	20.58
21	4.41	47	9.87	73	15.33	99	20.79
22	4.62	48	10.08	74	15.54	100	21.00
23	4.83	49	10.29	75	15.75	200	42.00
24	5.04	50	10.50	76	15.96	400	84.00
25	5.25	51	10.71	77	16.17	600	126.00
26	5.46	52	10.92	78	16.38	1000	210.00

	£.np.		£.np.		£.np.		£.np.
1	21½	27	5.80½	53	11.39½	79	16.98½
2	43	28	6.02	54	11.61	80	17.20
3	64½	29	6.23½	55	11.82½	81	17.41½
4	86	30	6.45	56	12.04	82	17.63
5	1.07½	31	6.66½	57	12.25½	83	17.84½
6	1.29	32	6.88	58	12.47	84	18.06
7	1.50½	33	7.09½	59	12.68½	85	18.27½
8	1.72	34	7.31	60	12.90	86	18.49
9	1.93½	35	7.52½	61	13.11½	87	18.70½
10	2.15	36	7.74	62	13.33	88	18.92
11	2.36½	37	7.95½	63	13.54½	89	19.13½
12	2.58	38	8.17	64	13.76	90	19.35
13	2.79½	39	8.38½	65	13.97½	91	19.56½
14	3.01	40	8.60	66	14.19	92	19.78
15	3.22½	41	8.81½	67	14.40½	93	19.99½
16	3.44	42	9.03	68	14.62	94	20.21
17	3.65½	43	9.24½	69	14.83½	95	20.42½
18	3.87	44	9.46	70	15.05	96	20.64
19	4.08½	45	9.67½	71	15.26½	97	20.85½
20	4.30	46	9.89	72	15.48	98	21.07
21	4.51½	47	10.10½	73	15.69½	99	21.28½
22	4.73	48	10.32	74	15.91	100	21.50
23	4.94½	49	10.53½	75	16.12½	200	43.00
24	5.16	50	10.75	76	16.34	400	86.00
25	5.37½	51	10.96½	77	16.55½	600	129.00
26	5.59	52	11.18	78	16.77	1000	215.00

	£.np.		£.np.		£.np.		£.np.
1	22	27	5.94	53	11.66	79	17.38
2	44	28	6.16	54	11.88	80	17.60
3	66	29	6.38	55	12.10	81	17.82
4	88	30	6.60	56	12.32	82	18.04
5	1.10	31	6.82	57	12.54	83	18.26
6	1.32	32	7.04	58	12.76	84	18.48
7	1.54	33	7.26	59	12.98	85	18.70
8	1.76	34	7.48	60	13.20	86	18.92
9	1.98	35	7.70	61	13.42	87	19.14
10	2.20	36	7.92	62	13.64	88	19.36
11	2.42	37	8.14	63	13.86	89	19.58
12	2.64	38	8.36	64	14.08	90	19.80
13	2.86	39	8.58	65	14.30	91	20.02
14	3.08	40	8.80	66	14.52	92	20.24
15	3.30	41	9.02	67	14.74	93	20.46
16	3.52	42	9.24	68	14.96	94	20.68
17	3.74	43	9.46	69	15.18	95	20.90
18	3.96	44	9.68	70	15.40	96	21.12
19	4.18	45	9.90	71	15.62	97	21.34
20	4.40	46	10.12	72	15.84	98	21.56
21	4.62	47	10.34	73	16.06	99	21.78
22	4.84	48	10.56	74	16.28	100	22.00
23	5.06	49	10.78	75	16.50	200	44.00
24	5.28	50	11.00	76	16.72	400	88.00
25	5.50	51	11.22	77	16.94	600	132.00
26	5.72	52	11.44	78	17.16	1000	220.00

	£.np.		£.np.		£.np.		£.np.
1	22½	27	6.07½	53	11.92½	79	17.77½
2	45	28	6.30	54	12.15	80	18.00
3	67½	29	6.52½	55	12.37½	81	18.22½
4	90	30	6.75	56	12.60	82	18.45
5	1.12½	31	6.97½	57	12.82½	83	18.67½
6	1.35	32	7.20	58	13.05	84	18.90
7	1.57½	33	7.42½	59	13.27½	85	19.12½
8	1.80	34	7.65	60	13.50	86	19.35
9	2.02½	35	7.87½	61	13.72½	87	19.57½
10	2.25	36	8.10	62	13.95	88	19.80
11	2.47½	37	8.32½	63	14.17½	89	20.02½
12	2.70	38	8.55	64	14.40	90	20.25
13	2.92½	39	8.77½	65	14.62½	91	20.47½
14	3.15	40	9.00	66	14.85	92	20.70
15	3.37½	41	9.22½	67	15.07½	93	20.92½
16	3.60	42	9.45	68	15.30	94	21.15
17	3.82½	43	9.67½	69	15.52½	95	21.37½
18	4.05	44	9.90	70	15.75	96	21.60
19	4.27½	45	10.12½	71	15.97½	97	21.82½
20	4.50	46	10.35	72	16.20	98	22.05
21	4.72½	47	10.57½	73	16.42½	99	22.27½
22	4.95	48	10.80	74	16.65	100	22.50
23	5.17½	49	11.02½	75	16.87½	200	45.00
24	5.40	50	11.25	76	17.10	400	90.00
25	5.62½	51	11.47½	77	17.32½	600	135.00
26	5.85	52	11.70	78	17.55	1000	225.00

23 NEW PENCE

	£.np.		£.np.		£.np.		£.np.
1	23	27	6.21	53	12.19	79	18.17
2	46	28	6.44	54	12.42	80	18.40
3	69	29	6.67	55	12.65	81	18.63
4	92	30	6.90	56	12.88	82	18.86
5	1.15	31	7.13	57	13.11	83	19.09
6	1.38	32	7.36	58	13.34	84	19.32
7	1.61	33	7.59	59	13.57	85	19.55
8	1.84	34	7.82	60	13.80	86	19.78
9	2.07	35	8.05	61	14.03	87	20.01
10	2.30	36	8.28	62	14.26	88	20.24
11	2.53	37	8.51	63	14.49	89	20.47
12	2.76	38	8.74	64	14.72	90	20.70
13	2.99	39	8.97	65	14.95	91	20.93
14	3.22	40	9.20	66	15.18	92	21.16
15	3.45	41	9.43	67	15.41	93	21.39
16	3.68	42	9.66	68	15.64	94	21.62
17	3.91	43	9.89	69	15.87	95	21.85
18	4.14	44	10.12	70	16.10	96	22.08
19	4.37	45	10.35	71	16.33	97	22.31
20	4.60	46	10.58	72	16.56	98	22.54
21	4.83	47	10.81	73	16.79	99	22.77
22	5.06	48	11.04	74	17.02	100	23.00
23	5.29	49	11.27	75	17.25	200	46.00
24	5.52	50	11.50	76	17.48	400	92.00
25	5.75	51	11.73	77	17.71	600	138.00
26	5.98	52	11.96	78	17.94	1000	230.00

4

23½ NEW PENCE

	£.np.		£.np.		£.np.		£.np.
1	23½	27	6.34½	53	12.45½	79	18.56½
2	47	28	6.58	54	12.69	80	18.80
3	70½	29	6.81½	55	12.92½	81	19.03½
4	94	30	7.05	56	13.16	82	19.27
5	1.17½	31	7.28½	57	13.39½	83	19.50½
6	1.41	32	7.52	58	13.63	84	19.74
7	1.64½	33	7.75½	59	13.86½	85	19.97½
8	1.88	34	7.99	60	14.10	86	20.21
9	2.11½	35	8.22½	61	14.33½	87	20.44½
10	2.35	36	8.46	62	14.57	88	20.68
11	2.58½	37	8.69½	63	14.80½	89	20.91½
12	2.82	38	8.93	64	15.04	90	21.15
13	3.05½	39	9.16½	65	15.27½	91	21.38½
14	3.29	40	9.40	66	15.51	92	21.62
15	3.52½	41	9.63½	67	15.74½	93	21.85½
16	3.76	42	9.87	68	15.98	94	22.09
17	3.99½	43	10.10½	69	16.21½	95	22.32½
18	4.23	44	10.34	70	16.45	96	22.56
19	4.46½	45	10.57½	71	16.68½	97	22.79½
20	4.70	46	10.81	72	16.92	98	23.03
21	4.93½	47	11.04½	73	17.15½	99	23.26½
22	5.17	48	11.28	74	17.39	100	23.50
23	5.40½	49	11.51½	75	17.62½	200	47 00
24	5.64	50	11.75	76	17.86	400	94 00
25	5.87½	51	11.98½	77	18.09½	600	141.00
26	6.11	52	12.22	78	18.33	1000	235.00

24 NEW PENCE

	£.np.		£.np.		£.np.		£.np.
1	24	27	6.48	53	12.72	79	18.96
2	48	28	6.72	54	12.96	80	19.20
3	72	29	6.96	55	13.20	81	19.44
4	96	30	7.20	56	13.44	82	19.68
5	1.20	31	7.44	57	13.68	83	19.92
6	1.44	32	7.68	58	13.92	84	20.16
7	1.68	33	7.92	59	14.16	85	20.40
8	1.92	34	8.16	60	14.40	86	20.64
9	2.16	35	8.40	61	14.64	87	20.88
10	2.40	36	8.64	62	14.88	88	21.12
11	2.64	37	8.88	63	15.12	89	21.36
12	2.88	38	9.12	64	15.36	90	21.60
13	3.12	39	9.36	65	15.60	91	21.84
14	3.36	40	9.60	66	15.84	92	22.08
15	3.60	41	9.84	67	16.08	93	22.32
16	3.84	42	10.08	68	16.32	94	22.56
17	4.08	43	10.32	69	16 56	95	22.80
18	4.32	44	10.56	70	16.80	96	23.04
19	4.56	45	10.80	71	17.04	97	23.28
20	4.80	46	11.04	72	17.28	98	23.52
21	5.04	47	11.28	73	17.52	99	23.76
22	5.28	48	11.52	74	17.76	100	24.00
23	5.52	49	11.76	75	18.00	200	48.00
24	5.76	50	12.00	76	18.24	400	96.00
25	6.00	51	12.24	77	18.48	600	144.00
26	6.24	52	12.48	78	18.72	1000	240.00

	£.np.		£.np.		£.np.		£.np.
1	24½	27	6.61½	53	12.98½	79	19.35½
2	49	28	6.86	54	13.23	80	19.60
3	73½	29	7.10½	55	13.47½	81	19.84½
4	98	30	7.35	56	13.72	82	20.09
5	1.22½	31	7.59½	57	13.96½	83	20.33½
6	1.47	32	7.84	58	14.21	84	20.58
7	1.71½	33	8.08½	59	14.45½	85	20.82½
8	1.96	34	8.33	60	14.70	86	21.07
9	2.20½	35	8.57½	61	14.94½	87	21.31½
10	2.45	36	8.82	62	15.19	88	21.56
11	2.69½	37	9.06½	63	15.43½	89	21.80½
12	2.94	38	9.31	64	15.68	90	22.05
13	3.18½	39	9.55½	65	15.92½	91	22.29½
14	3.43	40	9.80	66	16.17	92	22.54
15	3.67½	41	10.04½	67	16.41½	93	22.78½
16	3.92	42	10.29	68	16.66	94	23.03
17	4.16½	43	10.53½	69	16.90½	95	23.27½
18	4.41	44	10.78	70	17.15	96	23.52
19	4.65½	45	11.02½	71	17.39½	97	23.76½
20	4.90	46	11.27	72	17.64	98	24.01
21	5.14½	47	11.51½	73	17.88½	99	24.25½
22	5.39	48	11.76	74	18.13	100	24.50
23	5.63½	49	12.00½	75	18.37½	200	49.00
24	5.88	50	12.25	76	18.62	400	98.00
25	6.12½	51	12.49½	77	18.86½	600	147.00
26	6.37	52	12.74	78	19.11	1000	245.00

25 NEW PENCE

	£.np.		£.np.		£.np.		£.np.
1	25	27	6.75	53	13.25	79	19.75
2	50	28	7.00	54	13.50	80	20.00
3	75	29	7.25	55	13.75	81	20.25
4	1.00	30	7.50	56	14.00	82	20.50
5	1.25	31	7.75	57	14.25	83	20.75
6	1.50	32	8.00	58	14.50	84	21.00
7	1.75	33	8.25	59	14.75	85	21.25
8	2.00	34	8.50	60	15.00	86	21.50
9	2.25	35	8.75	61	15.25	87	21.75
10	2.50	36	9.00	62	15.50	88	22.00
11	2.75	37	9.25	63	15.75	89	22.25
12	3.00	38	9.50	64	16.00	90	22.50
13	3.25	39	9.75	65	16.25	91	22.75
14	3.50	40	10.00	66	16.50	92	23.00
15	3.75	41	10.25	67	16.75	93	23.25
16	4.00	42	10.50	68	17.00	94	23.50
17	4.25	43	10.75	69	17.25	95	23.75
18	4.50	44	11.00	70	17.50	96	24.00
19	4.75	45	11.25	71	17.75	97	24.25
20	5.00	46	11.50	72	18.00	98	24.50
21	5.25	47	11.75	73	18.25	99	24.75
22	5.50	48	12.00	74	18.50	100	25.00
23	5.75	49	12.25	75	18.75	200	50.00
24	6.00	50	12.50	76	19.00	400	100.00
25	6.25	51	12.75	77	19.25	600	150.00
26	6.50	52	13.00	78	19.50	1000	250.00

	£.np.		£.np.		£.np.		£.np.
1	26	27	7.02	53	13.78	79	20.54
2	52	28	7.28	54	14.04	80	20.80
3	78	29	7.54	55	14.30	81	21.06
4	1.04	30	7.80	56	14.56	82	21.32
5	1.30	31	8.06	57	14.82	83	21.58
6	1.56	32	8.32	58	15.08	84	21.84
7	1.82	33	8.58	59	15.34	85	22.10
8	2.08	34	8.84	60	15.60	86	22.36
9	2.34	35	9.10	61	15.86	87	22.62
10	2.60	36	9.36	62	16.12	88	22.88
11	2.86	37	9.62	63	16.38	89	23.14
12	3.12	38	9.88	64	16.64	90	23.40
13	3.38	39	10.14	65	16.90	91	23.66
14	3.64	40	10.40	66	17.16	92	23.92
15	3.90	41	10.66	67	17.42	93	24.18
16	4.16	42	10.92	68	17.68	94	24.44
17	4.42	43	11.18	69	17.94	95	24.70
18	4.68	44	11.44	70	18.20	96	24.96
19	4.94	45	11.70	71	18.46	97	25.22
20	5.20	46	11.96	72	18.72	98	25.48
21	5.46	47	12.22	73	18.98	99	25.74
22	5.72	48	12.48	74	19.24	100	26.00
23	5.98	49	12.74	75	19.50	200	52.00
24	6.24	50	13.00	76	19.76	400	104.00
25	6.50	51	13.26	77	20.02	600	156.00
26	6.76	52	13.52	78	20.28	1000	260.00

	£.np.		£.np.		£.np.		£.np.
1	27	27	7.29	53	14.31	79	21.33
2	54	28	7.56	54	14.58	80	21.60
3	81	29	7.83	55	14.85	81	21.87
4	1.08	30	8.10	56	15.12	82	22.14
5	1.35	31	8.37	57	15.39	83	22.41
6	1.62	32	8.64	58	15.66	84	22.68
7	1.89	33	8.91	59	15.93	85	22.95
8	2.16	34	9.18	60	16.20	86	23.22
9	2.43	35	9.45	61	16.47	87	23.49
10	2.70	36	9.72	62	16.74	88	23.76
11	2.97	37	9.99	63	17.01	89	24.03
12	3.24	38	10.26	64	17.28	90	24.30
13	3.51	39	10.53	65	17.55	91	24.57
14	3.78	40	10.80	66	17.82	92	24.84
15	4.05	41	11.07	67	18.09	93	25.11
16	4.32	42	11.34	68	18.36	94	25.38
17	4.59	43	11.61	69	18.63	95	25.65
18	4.86	44	11.88	70	18.90	96	25.92
19	5.13	45	12.15	71	19.17	97	26.19
20	5.40	46	12.42	72	19.44	98	26.46
21	5.67	47	12.69	73	19.71	99	26.73
22	5.94	48	12.96	74	19.98	100	27.00
23	6.21	49	13.23	75	20.25	200	54.00
24	6.48	50	13.50	76	20.52	400	108.00
25	6.75	51	13.77	77	20.79	600	162.00
26	7.02	52	14.04	78	21.06	1000	270.00

	£.np.		£.np.		£.np.		£.np.
1	28	27	7.56	53	14.84	79	22.12
2	56	28	7.84	54	15.12	80	22.40
3	84	29	8.12	55	15.40	81	22.68
4	1.12	30	8.40	56	15.68	82	22.96
5	1.40	31	8.68	57	15.96	83	23.24
6	1.68	32	8.96	58	16.24	84	23.52
7	1.96	33	9.24	59	16.52	85	23.80
8	2.24	34	9.52	60	16.80	86	24.08
9	2.52	35	9.80	61	17.08	87	24.36
10	2.80	36	10.08	62	17.36	88	24.64
11	3.08	37	10.36	63	17.64	89	24.92
12	3.36	38	10.64	64	17.92	90	25.20
13	3.64	39	10.92	65	18.20	91	25.48
14	3.92	40	11.20	66	18.48	92	25.76
15	4.20	41	11.48	67	18.76	93	26.04
16	4.48	42	11.76	68	19.04	94	26.32
17	4.76	43	12.04	69	19.32	95	26.60
18	5.04	44	12.32	70	19.60	96	26.88
19	5.32	45	12.60	71	19.88	97	27.16
20	5.60	46	12.88	72	20.16	98	27.44
21	5.88	47	13.16	73	20.44	99	27.72
22	6.16	48	13.44	74	20.72	100	28.00
23	6.44	49	13.72	75	21.00	200	56.00
24	6.72	50	14.00	76	21.28	400	112.00
25	7.00	51	14.28	77	21.56	600	168.00
26	7.28	52	14.56	78	21.84	1000	280.00

	£.np.		£.np.		£.np.		£.np.
1	29	27	7.83	53	15.37	79	22.91
2	58	28	8.12	54	15.66	80	23.20
3	87	29	8.41	55	15.95	81	23.49
4	1.16	30	8.70	56	16.24	82	23.78
5	1.45	31	8.99	57	16.53	83	24.07
6	1.74	32	9.28	58	16.82	84	24.36
7	2.03	33	9.57	59	17.11	85	24.65
8	2.32	34	9.86	60	17.40	86	24.94
9	2.61	35	10.15	61	17.69	87	25.23
10	2.90	36	10.44	62	17.98	88	25.52
11	3.19	37	10.73	63	18.27	89	25.81
12	3.48	38	11.02	64	18.56	90	26.10
13	3.77	39	11.31	65	18.85	91	26.39
14	4.06	40	11.60	66	19.14	92	26.68
15	4.35	41	11.89	67	19.43	93	26.97
16	4.64	42	12.18	68	19.72	94	27.26
17	4.93	43	12.47	69	20.01	95	27.55
18	5.22	44	12.76	70	20.30	96	27.84
19	5.51	45	13.05	71	20.59	97	28.13
20	5.80	46	13.34	72	20.88	98	28.42
21	6.09	47	13.63	73	21.17	99	28.71
22	6.38	48	13.92	74	21.46	100	29.00
23	6.67	49	14.21	75	21.75	200	58.00
24	6.96	50	14.50	76	22.04	400	116.00
25	7.25	51	14.79	77	22.33	600	174.00
26	7.54	52	15.08	78	22.62	1000	290.00

	£.np.		£.np.		£.np.		£.np.
1	30	27	8.10	53	15.90	79	23.70
2	60	28	8.40	54	16.20	80	24.00
3	90	29	8.70	55	16.50	81	24.30
4	1.20	30	9.00	56	16.80	82	24.60
5	1.50	31	9.30	57	17.10	83	24.90
6	1.80	32	9.60	58	17.40	84	25.20
7	2.10	33	9.90	59	17.70	85	25.50
8	2.40	34	10.20	60	18.00	86	25.80
9	2.70	35	10.50	61	18.30	87	26.10
10	3.00	36	10.80	62	18.60	88	26.40
11	3.30	37	11.10	63	18.90	89	26.70
12	3.60	38	11.40	64	19.20	90	27.00
13	3.90	39	11.70	65	19.50	91	27.30
14	4.20	40	12.00	66	19.80	92	27.60
15	4.50	41	12.30	67	20.10	93	27.90
16	4.80	42	12.60	68	20.40	94	28.20
17	5.10	43	12.90	69	20.70	95	28.50
18	5.40	44	13.20	70	21.00	96	28.80
19	5.70	45	13.50	71	21.30	97	29.10
20	6.00	46	13.80	72	21.60	98	29.40
21	6.30	47	14.10	73	21.90	99	29.70
22	6.60	48	14.40	74	22.20	100	30.00
23	6.90	49	14.70	75	22.50	200	60.00
24	7.20	50	15.00	76	22.80	400	120.00
25	7.50	51	15.30	77	23.10	600	180.00
26	7.80	52	15.60	78	23.40	1000	300.00

	£.np.		£.np.		£.np.		£.np.
1	31	27	8.37	53	16.43	79	24.49
2	62	28	8.68	54	16.74	80	24.80
3	93	29	8.99	55	17.05	81	25.11
4	1.24	30	9.30	56	17.36	82	25.42
5	1.55	31	9.61	57	17.67	83	25.73
6	1.86	32	9.92	58	17.98	84	26.04
7	2.17	33	10.23	59	18.29	85	26.35
8	2.48	34	10.54	60	18.60	86	26.66
9	2.79	35	10.85	61	18.91	87	26.97
10	3.10	36	11.16	62	19.22	88	27.28
11	3.41	37	11.47	63	19.53	89	27.59
12	3.72	38	11.78	64	19.84	90	27.90
13	4.03	39	12.09	65	20.15	91	28.21
14	4.34	40	12.40	66	20.46	92	28.52
15	4.65	41	12.71	67	20.77	93	28.83
16	4.96	42	13.02	68	21.08	94	29.14
17	5.27	43	13.33	69	21.39	95	29.45
18	5.58	44	13.64	70	21.70	96	29.76
19	5.89	45	13.95	71	22.01	97	30.07
20	6.20	46	14.26	72	22.32	98	30.38
21	6.51	47	14.57	73	22.63	99	30.69
22	6.82	48	14.88	74	22.94	100	31.00
23	7.13	49	15.19	75	23.25	200	62.00
24	7.44	50	15.50	76	23.56	400	124.00
25	7.75	51	15.81	77	23.87	600	186.00
26	8.06	52	16.12	78	24.18	1,000	310.00

	£.np.		£.np.		£.np.		£.np.
1	32	27	8.64	53	16.96	79	25.28
2	64	28	8.96	54	17.28	80	25.60
3	96	29	9.28	55	17.60	81	25.92
4	1.28	30	9.60	56	17.92	82	26.24
5	1.60	31	9.92	57	18.24	83	26.56
6	1.92	32	10.24	58	18.56	84	26.88
7	2.24	33	10.56	59	18.88	85	27.20
8	2.56	34	10.88	60	19.20	86	27.52
9	2.88	35	11.20	61	19.52	87	27.84
10	3.20	36	11.52	62	19.84	88	28.16
11	3.52	37	11.84	63	20.16	89	28.48
12	3.84	38	12.16	64	20.48	90	28.80
13	4.16	39	12.48	65	20.80	91	29.12
14	4.48	40	12.80	66	21.12	92	29.44
15	4.80	41	13.12	67	21.44	93	29.76
16	5.12	42	13.44	68	21.76	94	30.08
17	5.44	43	13.76	69	22.08	95	30.40
18	5.76	44	14.08	70	22.40	96	30.72
19	6.08	45	14.40	71	22.72	97	31.04
20	6.40	46	14.72	72	23.04	98	31.36
21	6.72	47	15.04	73	23.36	99	31.68
22	7.04	48	15.36	74	23.68	100	32.00
23	7.36	49	15.68	75	24.00	200	64.00
24	7.68	50	16.00	76	24.32	400	128.00
25	8.00	51	16.32	77	24.64	600	192.00
26	8.32	52	16.64	78	24.96	1000	320.00

33 NEW PENCE

	£.np.		£.np.		£.np.		£.np.
1	33	27	8.91	53	17.49	79	26.07
2	·66	28	9.24	54	17.82	80	26.40
3	99	29	9.57	55	18.15	81	26.73
4	1.32	30	9.90	56	18.48	82	27.06
5	1.65	31	10.23	57	18.81	83	27.39
6	1.98	32	10.56	58	19.14	84	27.72
7	2.31	33	10.89	59	19.47	85	28.05
8	2.64	34	11.22	60	19.80	86	28.38
9	2.97	35	11.55	61	20.13	87	28.71
10	3.30	36	11.88	62	20.46	88	29.04
11	3.63	37	12.21	63	20.79	89	29.37
12	3.96	38	12.54	64	21.12	90	29.70
13	4.29	39	12.87	65	21.45	91	30.03
14	4.62	40	13.20	66	21.78	92	30.36
15	4.95	41	13.53	67	22.11	93	30.69
16	5.28	42	13.86	68	22.44	94	31.02
17	5.61	43	14.19	69	22.77	95	31.35
18	5.94	44	14.52	70	23.10	96	31.68
19	6.27	45	14.85	71	23.43	97	32.01
20	6.60	46	15.18	72	23.76	98	32.34
21	6.93	47	15.51	73	24.09	99	32.67
22	7.26	48	15.84	74	24.42	100	33.00
23	7.59	49	16.17	75	24.75	200	66.00
24	7.92	50	16.50	76	25.08	400	132.00
25	8.25	51	16.83	77	25.41	600	198.00
26	8.58	52	17.16	78	25.74	1000	330.00

	£.np.		£.np.		£.np.		£.np.
1	34	27	9.18	53	18.02	79	26.86
2	68	28	9.52	54	18.36	80	27.20
3	1.02	29	9.86	55	18.70	81	27.54
4	1.36	30	10.20	56	19.04	82	27.88
5	1.70	31	10.54	57	19.38	83	28.22
6	2.04	32	10.88	58	19.72	84	28.56
7	2.38	33	11.22	59	20.06	85	28.90
8	2.72	34	11.56	60	20.40	86	29.24
9	3.06	35	11.90	61	20.74	87	29.58
10	3.40	36	12.24	62	21.08	88	29.92
11	3.74	37	12.58	63	21.42	89	30.26
12	4.08	38	12.92	64	21.76	90	30.60
13	4.42	39	13.26	65	22.10	91	30.94
14	4.76	40	13.60	66	22.44	92	31.28
15	5.10	41	13.94	67	22.78	93	31.62
16	5.44	42	14.28	68	23.12	94	31.96
17	5.78	43	14.62	69	23.46	95	32.30
18	6.12	44	14.96	70	23.80	96	32.64
19	6.46	45	15.30	71	24.14	97	32.98
20	6.80	46	15.64	72	24.48	98	33.32
21	7.14	47	15.98	73	24.82	99	33.66
22	7.48	48	16.32	74	25.16	100	34.00
23	7.82	49	16.66	75	25.50	200	68.00
24	8.16	50	17.00	76	25.84	400	136.00
25	8.50	51	17.34	77	26.18	600	204.00
26	8.84	52	17.68	78	26.52	1000	340.00

	£.np.		£.np.		£.np.		£.np.
1	35	27	9.45	53	18.55	79	27.65
2	70	28	9.80	54	18.90	80	28.00
3	1.05	29	10.15	55	19.25	81	28.35
4	1.40	30	10.50	56	19.60	82	28.70
5	1.75	31	10.85	57	19.95	83	29.05
6	2.10	32	11.20	58	20.30	84	29.40
7	2.45	33	11.55	59	20.65	85	29.75
8	2.80	34	11.90	60	21.00	86	30.10
9	3.15	35	12.25	61	21.35	87	30.45
10	3.50	36	12.60	62	21.70	88	30.80
11	3.85	37	12.95	63	22.05	89	31.15
12	4.20	38	13.30	64	22.40	90	31.50
13	4.55	39	13.65	65	22.75	91	31.85
14	4.90	40	14.00	66	23.10	92	32.20
15	5.25	41	14.35	67	23.45	93	32.55
16	5.60	42	14.70	68	23.80	94	32.90
17	5.95	43	15.05	69	24.15	95	33.25
18	6.30	44	15.40	70	24.50	96	33.60
19	6.65	45	15.75	71	24.85	97	33.95
20	7.00	46	16.10	72	25.20	98	34.30
21	7.35	47	16.45	73	25.55	99	34.65
22	7.70	48	16.80	74	25.90	100	35.00
23	8.05	49	17.15	75	26.25	200	70.00
24	8.40	50	17.50	76	26.60	400	140.00
25	8.75	51	17.85	77	26.95	600	210.00
26	9.10	52	18.20	78	27.30	1000	350.00

36 NEW PENCE

	£.np.		£.np.		£.np.		£.np.
1	36	27	9.72	53	19.08	79	28.44
2	72	28	10.08	54	19.44	80	28.80
3	1.08	29	10.44	55	19.80	81	29.16
4	1.44	30	10.80	56	20.16	82	29.52
5	1.80	31	11.16	57	20.52	83	29.88
6	2.16	32	11.52	58	20.88	84	30.24
7	2.52	33	11.88	59	21.24	85	30.60
8	2.88	34	12.24	60	21.60	86	30.96
9	3.24	35	12.60	61	21.96	87	31.32
10	3.60	36	12.96	62	22.32	88	31.68
11	3.96	37	13.32	63	22.68	89	32.04
12	4.32	38	13.68	64	23.04	90	32.40
13	4.68	39	14.04	65	23.40	91	32.76
14	5.04	40	14.40	66	23.76	92	33.12
15	5.40	41	14.76	67	24.12	93	33.48
16	5.76	42	15.12	68	24.48	94	33.84
17	6.12	43	15.48	69	24.84	95	34.20
18	6.48	44	15.84	70	25.20	96	34.56
19	6.84	45	16.20	71	25.56	97	34.92
20	7.20	46	16.56	72	25.92	98	35.28
21	7.56	47	16.92	73	26.28	99	35.64
22	7.92	48	17.28	74	26.64	100	36.00
23	8.28	49	17.64	75	27.00	200	72.00
24	8.64	50	18.00	76	27.36	400	144.00
25	9.00	51	18.36	77	27.72	600	216.00
26	9.36	52	18.72	78	28.08	1000	360.00

37 NEW PENCE

	£.np.		£.np.		£.np.		£.np.
1	37	27	9.99	53	19.61	79	29.23
2	74	28	10.36	54	19.98	80	29.60
3	1.11	29	10.73	55	20.35	81	29.97
4	1.48	30	11.10	56	20.72	82	30.34
5	1.85	31	11.47	57	21.09	83	30.71
6	2.22	32	11.84	58	21.46	84	31.08
7	2.59	33	12.21	59	21.83	85	31.45
8	2.96	34	12.58	60	22.20	86	31.82
9	3.33	35	12.95	61	22.57	87	32.19
10	3.70	36	13.32	62	22.94	88	32.56
11	4.07	37	13.69	63	23.31	89	32.93
12	4.44	38	14.06	64	23.68	90	33.30
13	4.81	39	14.43	65	24.05	91	33.67
14	5.18	40	14.80	66	24.42	92	34.04
15	5.55	41	15.17	67	24.79	93	34.41
16	5.92	42	15.54	68	25.16	94	34.78
17	6.29	43	15.91	69	25.53	95	35.15
18	6.66	44	16.28	70	25.90	96	35.52
19	7.03	45	16.65	71	26.27	97	35.89
20	7.40	46	17.02	72	26.64	98	36.26
21	7.77	47	17.39	73	27.01	99	36.63
22	8.14	48	17.76	74	27.38	100	37.00
23	8.51	49	18.13	75	27.75	200	74.00
24	8.88	50	18.50	76	28.12	400	148.00
25	9.25	51	18.87	77	28.49	600	222.00
26	9.62	52	19.24	78	28.86	1000	370.00

5

38 NEW PENCE

	£.np.		£.np.		£.np.		£.np.
1	38	27	10.26	53	20.14	79	30.02
2	76	28	10.64	54	20.52	80	30.40
3	1.14	29	11.02	55	20.90	81	30.78
4	1.52	30	11.40	56	21.28	82	31.16
5	1.90	31	11.78	57	21.66	83	31.54
6	2.28	32	12.16	58	22.04	84	31.92
7	2.66	33	12.54	59	22.42	85	32.30
8	3.04	34	12.92	60	22.80	86	32.68
9	3.42	35	13.30	61	23.18	87	33.06
10	3.80	36	13.68	62	23.56	88	33.44
11	4.18	37	14.06	63	23.94	89	33.82
12	4.56	38	14.44	64	24.32	90	34.20
13	4.94	39	14.82	65	24.70	91	34.58
14	5.32	40	15.20	66	25.08	92	34.96
15	5.70	41	15.58	67	25.46	93	35.34
16	6.08	42	15.96	68	25.84	94	35.72
17	6.46	43	16.34	69	26.22	95	36.10
18	6.84	44	16.72	70	26.60	96	36.48
19	7.22	45	17.10	71	26.98	97	36.86
20	7.60	46	17.48	72	27.36	98	37.24
21	7.98	47	17.86	73	27.74	99	37.62
22	8.36	48	18.24	74	28.12	100	38.00
23	8.74	49	18.62	75	28.50	200	76.00
24	9.12	50	19.00	76	28.88	400	152.00
25	9.50	51	19.38	77	29.26	600	228.00
26	9.88	52	19.76	78	29.64	1000	380.00

39 NEW PENCE

	£.np.		£.np.		£.np.		£.np.
1	39	27	10.53	53	20.67	79	30.81
2	78	28	10.92	54	21.06	80	31.20
3	1.17	29	11.31	55	21.45	81	31.59
4	1.56	30	11.70	56	21.84	82	31.98
5	1.95	31	12.09	57	22.23	83	32.37
6	2.34	32	12.48	58	22.62	84	32.76
7	2.73	33	12.87	59	23.01	85	33.15
8	3.12	34	13.26	60	23.40	86	33.54
9	3.51	35	13.65	61	23.79	87	33.93
10	3.90	36	14.04	62	24.18	88	34.32
11	4.29	37	14.43	63	24.57	89	34.71
12	4.68	38	14.82	64	24.96	90	35.10
13	5.07	39	15.21	65	25.35	91	35.49
14	5.46	40	15.60	66	25.74	92	35.88
15	5.85	41	15.99	67	26.13	93	36.27
16	6.24	42	16.38	68	26.52	94	36.66
17	6.63	43	16.77	69	26.91	95	37.05
18	7.02	44	17.16	70	27.30	96	37.44
19	7.41	45	17.55	71	27.69	97	37.83
20	7.80	46	17.94	72	28.08	98	38.22
21	8.19	47	18.33	73	28.47	99	38.61
22	8.58	48	18.72	74	28.86	100	39.00
23	8.97	49	19.11	75	29.25	200	78.00
24	9.36	50	19.50	76	29.64	400	156.00
25	9.75	51	19.89	77	30.03	600	234.00
26	10.14	52	20.28	78	30.42	1000	390.00

40 NEW PENCE

	£.np.		£.np.		£.np.		£.np.
1	40	27	10.80	53	21.20	79	31.60
2	80	28	11.20	54	21.60	80	32.00
3	1.20	29	11.60	55	22.00	81	32.40
4	1.60	30	12.00	56	22.40	82	32.80
5	2.00	31	12.40	57	22.80	83	33.20
6	2.40	32	12.80	58	23.20	84	33.60
7	2.80	33	13.20	59	23.60	85	34.00
8	3.20	34	13.60	60	24.00	86	34.40
9	3.60	35	14.00	61	24.40	87	34.80
10	4.00	36	14.40	62	24.80	88	35.20
11	4.40	37	14.80	63	25.20	89	35.60
12	4.80	38	15.20	64	25.60	90	36.00
13	5.20	39	15.60	65	26.00	91	36.40
14	5.60	40	16.00	66	26.40	92	36.80
15	6.00	41	16.40	67	26.80	93	37.20
16	6.40	42	16.80	68	27.20	94	37.60
17	6.80	43	17.20	69	27.60	95	38.00
18	7.20	44	17.60	70	28.00	96	38.40
19	7.60	45	18.00	71	28.40	97	38.80
20	8.00	46	18.40	72	28.80	98	39.20
21	8.40	47	18.80	73	29.20	99	39.60
22	8.80	48	19.20	74	29.60	100	40.00
23	9.20	49	19.60	75	30.00	200	80.00
24	9.60	50	20.00	76	30.40	400	160.00
25	10.00	51	20.40	77	30.80	600	240.00
26	10.40	52	20.80	78	31.20	1000	400.00

	£.np.		£.np.		£.np.		£.np.
1	41	27	11.07	53	21.73	79	32.39
2	82	28	11.48	54	22.14	80	32.80
3	1.23	29	11.89	55	22.55	81	33.21
4	1.64	30	12.30	56	22.96	82	33.62
5	2.05	31	12.71	57	23.37	83	34.03
6	2.46	32	13.12	58	23.78	84	34.44
7	2.87	33	13.53	59	24.19	85	34.85
8	3.28	34	13.94	60	24.60	86	35.26
9	3.69	35	14.35	61	25.01	87	35.67
10	4.10	36	14.76	62	25.42	88	36.08
11	4.51	37	15.17	63	25.83	89	36.49
12	4.92	38	15.58	64	26.24	90	36.90
13	5.33	39	15.99	65	26.65	91	37.31
14	5.74	40	16.40	66	27.06	92	37.72
15	6.15	41	16.81	67	27.47	93	38.13
16	6.56	42	17.22	68	27.88	94	38.54
17	6.97	43	17.63	69	28.29	95	38.95
18	7.38	44	18.04	70	28.70	96	39.36
19	7.79	45	18.45	71	29.11	97	39.77
20	8.20	46	18.86	72	29.52	98	40.18
21	8.61	47	19.27	73	29.93	99	40.59
22	9.02	48	19.68	74	30.34	100	41.00
23	9.43	49	20.09	75	30.75	200	82.00
24	9.84	50	20.50	76	31.16	400	164.00
25	10.25	51	20.91	77	31.57	600	246.00
26	10.66	52	21.32	78	31.98	1000	410.00

42 NEW PENCE

	£.np.		£.np.		£.np.		£.np.
1	42	27	11.34	53	22.26	79	33.18
2	84	28	11.76	54	22.68	80	33.60
3	1.26	29	12.18	55	23.10	81	34.02
4	1.68	30	12.60	56	23.52	82	34.44
5	2.10	31	13.02	57	23.94	83	34.86
6	2.52	32	13.44	58	24.36	84	35.28
7	2.94	33	13.86	59	24.78	85	35.70
8	3.36	34	14.28	60	25.20	86	36.12
9	3.78	35	14.70	61	25.62	87	36.54
10	4.20	36	15.12	62	26.04	88	36.96
11	4.62	37	15.54	63	26.46	89	37.38
12	5.04	38	15.96	64	26.88	90	37.80
13	5.46	39	16.38	65	27.30	91	38.22
14	5.88	40	16.80	66	27.72	92	38.64
15	6.30	41	17.22	67	28.14	93	39.06
16	6.72	42	17.64	68	28.56	94	39.48
17	7.14	43	18.06	69	28.98	95	39.90
18	7.56	44	18.48	70	29.40	96	40.32
19	7.98	45	18.90	71	29.82	97	40.74
20	8.40	46	19.32	72	30.24	98	41.16
21	8.82	47	19.74	73	30.66	99	41.58
22	9.24	48	20.16	74	31.08	100	42.00
23	9.66	49	20.58	75	31.50	200	84.00
24	10.08	50	21.00	76	31.92	400	168.00
25	10.50	51	21.42	77	32.34	600	252.00
26	10.92	52	21.84	78	32.76	1000	420.00

43 NEW PENCE

	£.np.		£.np.		£.np.		£.np.
1	43	27	11.61	53	22.79	79	33.97
2	86	28	12.04	54	23.22	80	34.40
3	1.29	29	12.47	55	23.65	81	34.83
4	1.72	30	12.90	56	24.08	82	35.26
5	2.15	31	13.33	57	24.51	83	35.69
6	2.58	32	13.76	58	24.94	84	36.12
7	3.01	33	14.19	59	25.37	85	36.55
8	3.44	34	14.62	60	25.80	86	36.98
9	3.87	35	15.05	61	26.23	87	37.41
10	4.30	36	15.48	62	26.66	88	37.84
11	4.73	37	15.91	63	27.09	89	38.27
12	5.16	38	16.34	64	27.52	90	38.70
13	5.59	39	16.77	65	27.95	91	39.13
14	6.02	40	17.20	66	28.38	92	39.56
15	6.45	41	17.63	67	28.81	93	39.99
16	6.88	42	18.06	68	29.24	94	40.42
17	7.31	43	18.49	69	29.67	95	40.85
18	7.74	44	18.92	70	30.10	96	41.28
19	8.17	45	19.35	71	30.53	97	41.71
20	8.60	46	19.78	72	30.96	98	42.14
21	9.03	47	20.21	73	31.39	99	42.57
22	9.46	48	20.64	74	31.82	100	43.00
23	9.89	49	21.07	75	32.25	200	86.00
24	10.32	50	21.50	76	32.68	400	172.00
25	10.75	51	21.93	77	33.11	600	258.00
26	11.18	52	22.36	78	33.54	1000	430.00

44 NEW PENCE

	£.np.		£.np.		£.np.		£.np.
1	44	27	11.88	53	23.32	79	34.76
2	88	28	12.32	54	23.76	80	35.20
3	1.32	29	12.76	55	24.20	81	35.64
4	1.76	30	13.20	56	24.64	82	36.08
5	2.20	31	13.64	57	25.08	83	36.52
6	2.64	32	14.08	58	25.52	84	36.96
7	3.08	33	14.52	59	25.96	85	37.40
8	3.52	34	14.96	60	26.40	86	37.84
9	3.96	35	15.40	61	26.84	87	38.28
10	4.40	36	15.84	62	27.28	88	38.72
11	4.84	37	16.28	63	27.72	89	39.16
12	5.28	38	16.72	64	28.16	90	39.60
13	5.72	39	17.16	65	28.60	91	40.04
14	6.16	40	17.60	66	29.04	92	40.48
15	6.60	41	18.04	67	29.48	93	40.92
16	7.04	42	18.48	68	29.92	94	41.36
17	7.48	43	18.92	69	30.36	95	41.80
18	7.92	44	19.36	70	30.80	96	42.24
19	8.36	45	19.80	71	31.24	97	42.68
20	8.80	46	20.24	72	31.68	98	43.12
21	9.24	47	20.68	73	32.12	99	43.56
22	9.68	48	21.12	74	32.56	100	44.00
23	10.12	49	21.56	75	33.00	200	88.00
24	10.56	50	22.00	76	33.44	400	176.00
25	11.00	51	22.44	77	33.88	600	264.00
26	11.44	52	22.88	78	34.32	1000	440.00

45 NEW PENCE

	£.np.		£.np.		£.np.		£.np.
1	45	27	12.15	53	23.85	79	35.55
2	90	28	12.60	54	24.30	80	36.00
3	1.35	29	13.05	55	24.75	81	36.45
4	1.80	30	13.50	56	25.20	82	36.90
5	2.25	31	13.95	57	25.65	83	37.35
6	2.70	32	14.40	58	26.10	84	37.80
7	3.15	33	14.85	59	26.55	85	38.25
8	3.60	34	15.30	60	27.00	86	38.70
9	4.05	35	15.75	61	27.45	87	39.15
10	4.50	36	16.20	62	27.90	88	39.60
11	4.95	37	16.65	63	28.35	89	40.05
12	5.40	38	17.10	64	28.80	90	40.50
13	5.85	39	17.55	65	29.25	91	40.95
14	6.30	40	18.00	66	29.70	92	41.40
15	6.75	41	18.45	67	30.15	93	41.85
16	7.20	42	18.90	68	30.60	94	42.30
17	7.65	43	19.35	69	31.05	95	42.75
18	8.10	44	19.80	70	31.50	96	43.20
19	8.55	45	20.25	71	31.95	97	43.65
20	9.00	46	20.70	72	32.40	98	44.10
21	9.45	47	21.15	73	32.85	99	44.55
22	9.90	48	21.60	74	33.30	100	45.00
23	10.35	49	22.05	75	33.75	200	90.00
24	10.80	50	22.50	76	34.20	400	180.00
25	11.25	51	22.95	77	34.65	600	270.00
26	11.70	52	23.40	78	35.10	1000	450.00

	£.np.		£.np.		£.np.		£.np.
1	46	27	12.42	53	24.38	79	36.34
2	92	28	12.88	54	24.84	80	36.80
3	1.38	29	13.34	55	25.30	81	37.26
4	1.84	30	13.80	56	25.76	82	37.72
5	2.30	31	14.26	57	26.22	83	38.18
6	2.76	32	14.72	58	26.68	84	38.64
7	3.22	33	15.18	59	27.14	85	39.10
8	3.68	34	15.64	60	27.60	86	39.56
9	4.14	35	16.10	61	28.06	87	40.02
10	4.60	36	16.56	62	28.52	88	40.48
11	5.06	37	17.02	63	28.98	89	40.94
12	5.52	38	17.48	64	29.44	90	41.40
13	5.98	39	17.94	65	29.90	91	41.86
14	6.44	40	18.40	66	30.36	92	42.32
15	6.90	41	18.86	67	30.82	93	42.78
16	7.36	42	19.32	68	31.28	94	43.24
17	7.82	43	19.78	69	31.74	95	43.70
18	8.28	44	20.24	70	32.20	96	44.16
19	8.74	45	20.70	71	32.66	97	44.62
20	9.20	46	21.16	72	33.12	98	45.08
21	9.66	47	21.62	73	33.58	99	45.54
22	10.12	48	22.08	74	34.04	100	46.00
23	10.58	49	22.54	75	34.50	200	92.00
24	11.04	50	23.00	76	34.96	400	184.00
25	11.50	51	23.46	77	35.42	600	276.00
26	11.96	52	23.92	78	35.88	1000	460.00

	£.np.		£.np.		£.np.		£.np.
1	47	27	12.69	53	24.91	79	37.13
2	94	28	13.16	54	25.38	80	37.60
3	1.41	29	13.63	55	25.85	81	38.07
4	1.88	30	14.10	56	26.32	82	38.54
5	2.35	31	14.57	57	26.79	83	39.01
6	2.82	32	15.04	58	27.26	84	39.48
7	3.29	33	15.51	59	27.73	85	39.95
8	3.76	34	15.98	60	28.20	86	40.42
9	4.23	35	16.45	61	28.67	87	40.89
10	4.70	36	16.92	62	29.14	88	41.36
11	5.17	37	17.39	63	29.61	89	41.83
12	5.64	38	17.86	64	30.08	90	42.30
13	6.11	39	18.33	65	30.55	91	42.77
14	6.58	40	18.80	66	31.02	92	43.24
15	7.05	41	19.27	67	31.49	93	43.71
16	7.52	42	19.74	68	31.96	94	44.18
17	7.99	43	20.21	69	32.43	95	44.65
18	8.46	44	20.68	70	32.90	96	45.12
19	8.93	45	21.15	71	33.37	97	45.59
20	9.40	46	21.62	72	33.84	98	46.06
21	9.87	47	22.09	73	34.31	99	46.53
22	10.34	48	22.56	74	34.78	100	47.00
23	10.81	49	23.03	75	35.25	200	94.00
24	11.28	50	23.50	76	35.72	400	188.00
25	11.75	51	23.97	77	36.19	600	282.00
26	12.22	52	24.44	78	36.66	1000	470.00

	£.np.		£.np.		£.np.		£.np.
1	48	27	12.96	53	25.44	79	37.92
2	96	28	13.44	54	25.92	80	38.40
3	1.44	29	13.92	55	26.40	81	38,88
4	1.92	30	14.40	56	26.88	82	39.36
5	2.40	31	14.88	57	27.36	83	39.84
6	2.88	32	15.36	58	27.84	84	40.32
7	3.36	33	15.84	59	28.32	85	40.80
8	3.84	34	16.32	60	28,80	86	41.28
9	4.32	35	16.80	61	29.28	87	41.76
10	4.80	36	17.28	62	29.76	88	42,24
11	5.28	37	17.76	63	30.24	89	42.72
12	5.76	38	18.24	64	30.72	90	43.20
13	6.24	39	18.72	65	31.20	91	43.68
14	6.72	40	19.20	66	31.68	92	44.16
15	7.20	41	19.68	67	32.16	93	44.64
16	7.68	42	20.16	68	32.64	94	45.12
17	8.16	43	20.64	69	33.12	95	45.60
18	8.64	44	21.12	70	33.60	96	46.08
19	9.12	45	21.60	71	34.08	97	46.56
20	9.60	46	22.08	72	34.56	98	47.04
21	10.08	47	22.56	73	35.04	99	47.52
22	10.56	48	23.04	74	35.52	100	48.00
23	11.04	49	23.52	75	36.00	200	96.00
24	11.52	50	24.00	76	36.48	400	192.00
25	12.00	51	24.48	77	36.96	600	288.00
26	12.48	52	24.96	78	37.44	1000	480.00

49 NEW PENCE

	£.np.		£.np.		£.np.		£.np.
1	49	27	13.23	53	25.97	79	38.71
2	98	28	13.72	54	26.46	80	39.20
3	1.47	29	14.21	55	26.95	81	39.69
4	1.96	30	14.70	56	27.44	82	40.18
5	2.45	31	15.19	57	27.93	83	40.67
6	2.94	32	15.68	58	28.42	84	41.16
7	3.43	33	16.17	59	28.91	85	41.65
8	3.92	34	16.66	60	29.40	86	42.14
9	4.41	35	17.15	61	29.89	87	42.63
10	4.90	36	17.64	62	30.38	88	43.12
11	5.39	37	18.13	63	30.87	89	43.61
12	5.88	38	18.62	64	31.36	90	44.10
13	6.37	39	19.11	65	31.85	91	44.59
14	6.86	40	19.60	66	32.34	92	45.08
15	7.35	41	20.09	67	32.83	93	45.57
16	7.84	42	20.58	68	33.32	94	46.06
17	8.33	43	21.07	69	33.81	95	46.55
18	8.82	44	21.56	70	34.30	96	47.04
19	9.31	45	22.05	71	34.79	97	47.53
20	9.80	46	22.54	72	35.28	98	48.02
21	10.29	47	23.03	73	35.77	99	48.51
22	10.78	48	23.52	74	36.26	100	49.00
23	11.27	49	24.01	75	36.75	200	98.00
24	11.76	50	24.50	76	37.24	400	196.00
25	12.25	51	24.99	77	37.73	600	294.00
26	12.74	52	25.48	78	38.22	1000	490.00

50 NEW PENCE

	£.np.		£.np.		£.np.		£.np.
1	50	27	13.50	53	26.50	79	39.50
2	1.00	28	14.00	54	27.00	80	40.00
3	1.50	29	14.50	55	27.50	81	40.50
4	2.00	30	15.00	56	28.00	82	41.00
5	2.50	31	15.50	57	28.50	83	41.50
6	3.00	32	16.00	58	29.00	84	42.00
7	3.50	33	16.50	59	29.50	85	42.50
8	4.00	34	17.00	60	30.00	86	43.00
9	4.50	35	17.50	61	30.50	87	43.50
10	5.00	36	18.00	62	31.00	88	44.00
11	5.50	37	18.50	63	31.50	89	44.50
12	6.00	38	19.00	64	32.00	90	45.00
13	6.50	39	19.50	65	32.50	91	45.50
14	7.00	40	20.00	66	33.00	92	46.00
15	7.50	41	20.50	67	33.50	93	46.50
16	8.00	42	21.00	68	34.00	94	47.00
17	8.50	43	21.50	69	34.50	95	47.50
18	9.00	44	22.00	70	35.00	96	48.00
19	9.50	45	22.50	71	35.50	97	48.50
20	10.00	46	23.00	72	36.00	98	49.00
21	10.50	47	23.50	73	36.50	99	49.50
22	11.00	48	24.00	74	37.00	100	50.00
23	11.50	49	24.50	75	37.50	200	100.00
24	12.00	50	25.00	76	38.00	400	200.00
25	12.50	51	25.50	77	38.50	600	300.00
26	13.00	52	26.00	78	39.00	1000	500.00

	£.np.		£.np.		£.np.		£.np.
1	51	27	13.77	53	27.03	79	40.29
2	1.02	28	14.28	54	27.54	80	40.80
3	1.53	29	14.79	55	28.05	81	41.31
4	2.04	30	15.30	56	28.56	82	41.82
5	2.55	31	15.81	57	29.07	83	42.33
6	3.06	32	16.32	58	29.58	84	42.84
7	3.57	33	16.83	59	30.09	85	43.35
8	4.08	34	17.34	60	30.60	86	43.86
9	4.59	35	17.85	61	31.11	87	44.37
10	5.10	36	18.36	62	31.62	88	44.88
11	5.61	37	18.87	63	32.13	89	45.39
12	6.12	38	19.38	64	32.64	90	45.90
13	6.63	39	19.89	65	33.15	91	46.41
14	7.14	40	20.40	66	33.66	92	46.92
15	7.65	41	20.91	67	34.17	93	47.43
16	8.16	42	21.42	68	34.68	94	47.94
17	8.67	43	21.93	69	35.19	95	48.45
18	9.18	44	22.44	70	35.70	96	48.96
19	9.69	45	22.95	71	36.21	97	49.47
20	10.20	46	23.46	72	36.72	98	49.98
21	10.71	47	23.97	73	37.23	99	50.49
22	11.22	48	24.48	74	37.74	100	51.00
23	11.73	49	24.99	75	38.25	200	102.00
24	12.24	50	25.50	76	38.76	400	204.00
25	12.75	51	26.01	77	39.27	600	306.00
26	13.26	52	26.52	78	39.78	1000	510.00

	£.np.		£.np.		£.np.		£.np.
1	52	27	14.04	53	27.56	79	41.08
2	1.04	28	14.56	54	28.08	80	41.60
3	1.56	29	15.08	55	28.60	81	42.12
4	2.08	30	15.60	56	29.12	82	42.64
5	2.60	31	16.12	57	29.64	83	43.16
6	3.12	32	16.64	58	30.16	84	43.68
7	3.64	33	17.16	59	30.68	85	44.20
8	4.16	34	17.68	60	31.20	86	44.72
9	4.68	35	18.20	61	31.72	87	45.24
10	5.20	36	18.72	62	32.24	88	45.76
11	5.72	37	19.24	63	32.76	89	46.28
12	6.24	38	19.76	64	33.28	90	46.80
13	6.76	39	20.28	65	33.80	91	47.32
14	7.28	40	20.80	66	34.32	92	47.84
15	7.80	41	21.32	67	34.84	93	48.36
16	8.32	42	21.84	68	35.36	94	48.88
17	8.84	43	22.36	69	35.88	95	49.40
18	9.36	44	22.88	70	36.40	96	49.92
19	9.88	45	23.40	71	36.92	97	50.44
20	10.40	46	23.92	72	37.44	98	50.96
21	10.92	47	24.44	73	37.96	99	51.48
22	11.44	48	24.96	74	38.48	100	52.00
23	11.96	49	25.48	75	39.00	200	104.00
24	12.48	50	26.00	76	39.52	400	208.00
25	13.00	51	26.52	77	40.04	600	312.00
26	13.52	52	27.04	78	40.56	1000	520.00

53 NEW PENCE

	£.np.		£.np.		£.np.		£.np.
1	53	27	14.31	53	28.09	79	41.87
2	1.06	28	14.84	54	28.62	80	42.40
3	1.59	29	15.37	55	29.15	81	42.93
4	2.12	30	15.90	56	29.68	82	43.46
5	2.65	31	16.43	57	30.21	83	43.99
6	3.18	32	16.96	58	30.74	84	44.52
7	3.71	33	17.49	59	31.27	85	45.05
8	4.24	34	18.02	60	31.80	86	45.58
9	4.77	35	18.55	61	32.33	87	46.11
10	5.30	36	19.08	62	32.86	88	46.64
11	5.83	37	19.61	63	33.39	89	47.17
12	6.36	38	20.14	64	33.92	90	47.70
13	6.89	39	20.67	65	34.45	91	48.23
14	7.42	40	21.20	66	34.98	92	48.76
15	7.95	41	21.73	67	35.51	93	49.29
16	8.48	42	22.26	68	36.04	94	49.82
17	9.01	43	22.79	69	36.57	95	50.35
18	9.54	44	23.32	70	37.10	96	50.88
19	10.07	45	23.85	71	37.63	97	51.41
20	10.60	46	24.38	72	38.16	98	51.94
21	11.13	47	24.91	73	38.69	99	52.47
22	11.66	48	25.44	74	39.22	100	53.00
23	12.19	49	25.97	75	39.75	200	106.00
24	12.72	50	26.50	76	40.28	400	212.00
25	13.25	51	27.03	77	40.81	600	318.00
26	13.78	52	27.56	78	41.34	1000	530.00

54 NEW PENCE

	£.np.		£.np.		£.np.		£.np.
1	54	27	14.58	53	28.62	79	42.66
2	1.08	28	15.12	54	29.16	80	43.20
3	1.62	29	15.66	55	29.70	81	43.74
4	2.16	30	16.20	56	30.24	82	44.28
5	2.70	31	16.74	57	30.78	83	44.82
6	3.24	32	17.28	58	31.32	84	45.36
7	3.78	33	17.82	59	31.86	85	45.90
8	4.32	34	18.36	60	32.40	86	46.44
9	4.86	35	18.90	61	32.94	87	46.98
10	5.40	36	19.44	62	33.48	88	47.52
11	5.94	37	19.98	63	34.02	89	48.06
12	6.48	38	20.52	64	34.56	90	48.60
13	7.02	39	21.06	65	35.10	91	49.14
14	7.56	40	21.60	66	35.64	92	49.68
15	8.10	41	22.14	67	36.18	93	50.22
16	8.64	42	22.68	68	36.72	94	50.76
17	9.18	43	23.22	69	37.26	95	51.30
18	9.72	44	23.76	70	37.80	96	51.84
19	10.26	45	24.30	71	38.34	97	52.38
20	10.80	46	24.84	72	38.88	98	52.92
21	11.34	47	25.38	73	39.42	99	53.46
22	11.88	48	25.92	74	39.96	100	54.00
23	12.42	49	26.46	75	40.50	200	108.00
24	12.96	50	27.00	76	41.04	400	216.00
25	13.50	51	27.54	77	41.58	600	324.00
26	14.04	52	28.08	78	42.12	1000	540.00

	£.np.		£.np.		£.np.		£.np.
1	55	27	14.85	53	29.15	79	43.45
2	1.10	28	15.40	54	29.70	80	44.00
3	1.65	29	15.95	55	30.25	81	44.55
4	2.20	30	16.50	56	30.80	82	45.10
5	2.75	31	17.05	57	31.35	83	45.65
6	3.30	32	17.60	58	31.90	84	46.20
7	3.85	33	18.15	59	32.45	85	46.75
8	4.40	34	18.70	60	33.00	86	47.30
9	4.95	35	19.25	61	33.55	87	47.85
10	5.50	36	19.80	62	34.10	88	48.40
11	6.05	37	20.35	63	34.65	89	48.95
12	6.60	38	20.90	64	35.20	90	49.50
13	7.15	39	21.45	65	35.75	91	50.05
14	7.70	40	22.00	66	36.30	92	50.60
15	8.25	41	22.55	67	36.85	93	51.15
16	8.80	42	23.10	68	37.40	94	51.70
17	9.35	43	23.65	69	37.95	95	52.25
18	9.90	44	24.20	70	38.50	96	52.80
19	10.45	45	24.75	71	39.05	97	53.35
20	11.00	46	25.30	72	39.60	98	53.90
21	11.55	47	25.85	73	40.15	99	54.45
22	12.10	48	26.40	74	40.70	100	55.00
23	12.65	49	26.95	75	41.25	200	110.00
24	13.20	50	27.50	76	41.80	400	220.00
25	13.75	51	28.05	77	42.35	600	330.00
26	14.30	52	28.60	78	42.90	1000	550.00

	£.np.		£.np.		£.np.		£.np.
1	56	27	15.12	53	29.68	79	44.24
2	1.12	28	15.68	54	30.24	80	44.80
3	1.68	29	16.24	55	30.80	81	45.36
4	2.24	30	16.80	56	31.36	82	45.92
5	2.80	31	17.36	57	31.92	83	46.48
6	3.36	32	17.92	58	32.48	84	47.04
7	3.92	33	18.48	59	33.04	85	47.60
8	4.48	34	19.04	60	33.60	86	48.16
9	5.04	35	19.60	61	34.16	87	48.72
10	5.60	36	20.16	62	34.72	88	49.28
11	6.16	37	20.72	63	35.28	89	49.84
12	6.72	38	21.28	64	35.84	90	50.40
13	7.28	39	21.84	65	36.40	91	50.96
14	7.84	40	22.40	66	36.96	92	51.52
15	8.40	41	22.96	67	37.52	93	52.08
16	8.96	42	23.52	68	38.08	94	52.64
17	9.52	43	24.08	69	38.64	95	53.20
18	10.08	44	24.64	70	39.20	96	53.76
19	10.64	45	25.20	71	39.76	97	54.32
20	11.20	46	25.76	72	40.32	98	54.88
21	11.76	47	26.32	73	40.88	99	55.44
22	12.32	48	26.88	74	41.44	100	56.00
23	12.88	49	27.44	75	42.00	200	112.00
24	13.44	50	28.00	76	42.56	400	224.00
25	14.00	51	28.56	77	43.12	600	336.00
26	14.56	52	29.12	78	43.68	1000	560.00

57 NEW PENCE

	£.np.		£.np.		£.np.		£.np.
1	57	27	15.39	53	30.21	79	45.03
2	1.14	28	15.96	54	30.78	80	45.60
3	1.71	29	16.53	55	31.35	81	46.17
4	2.28	30	17.10	56	31.92	82	46.74
5	2.85	31	17.67	57	32.49	83	47.31
6	3.42	32	18.24	58	33.06	84	47.88
7	3.99	33	18.81	59	33.63	85	48.45
8	4.56	34	19.38	60	34.20	86	49.02
9	5.13	35	19.95	61	34.77	87	49.59
10	5.70	36	20.52	62	35.34	88	50.16
11	6.27	37	21.09	63	35.91	89	50.73
12	6.84	38	21.66	64	36.48	90	51.30
13	7.41	39	22.23	65	37.05	91	51.87
14	7.98	40	22.80	66	37.62	92	52.44
15	8.55	41	23.37	67	38.19	93	53.01
16	9.12	42	23.94	68	38.76	94	53.58
17	9.69	43	24.51	69	39.33	95	54.15
18	10.26	44	25.08	70	39.90	96	54.72
19	10.83	45	25.65	71	40.47	97	55.29
20	11.40	46	26.22	72	41.04	98	55.86
21	11.97	47	26.79	73	41.61	99	56.43
22	12.54	48	27.36	74	42.18	100	57.00
23	13.11	49	27.93	75	42.75	200	114.00
24	13.68	50	28.50	76	43.32	400	228.00
25	14.25	51	29.07	77	43.89	600	342.00
26	14.82	52	29.64	78	44.46	1000	570.00

58 NEW PENCE

	£.np.		£.np.		£.np.		£.np.
1	58	27	15.66	53	30.74	79	45.82
2	1.16	28	16.24	54	31.32	80	46.40
3	1.74	29	16.82	55	31.90	81	46.98
4	2.32	30	17.40	56	32.48	82	47.56
5	2.90	31	17.98	57	33.06	83	48.14
6	3.48	32	18.56	58	33.64	84	48.72
7	4.06	33	19.14	59	34.22	85	49.30
8	4.64	34	19.72	60	34.80	86	49.88
9	5.22	35	20.30	61	35.38	87	50.46
10	5.80	36	20.88	62	35.96	88	51.04
11	6.38	37	21.46	63	36.54	89	51.62
12	6.96	38	22.04	64	37.12	90	52.20
13	7.54	39	22.62	65	37.70	91	52.78
14	8.12	40	23.20	66	38.28	92	53.36
15	8.70	41	23.78	67	38.86	93	53.94
16	9.28	42	24.36	68	39.44	94	54.52
17	9.86	43	24.94	69	40.02	95	55.10
18	10.44	44	25.52	70	40.60	96	55.68
19	11.02	45	26.10	71	41.18	97	56.26
20	11.60	46	26.68	72	41.76	98	56.84
21	12.18	47	27.26	73	42.34	99	57.42
22	12.76	48	27.84	74	42.92	100	58.00
23	13.34	49	28.42	75	43.50	200	116.00
24	13.92	50	29.00	76	44.08	400	232.00
25	14.50	51	29.58	77	44.66	600	348.00
26	15.08	52	30.16	78	45.24	1000	580.00

	£.np.		£.np.		£.np.		£.np.
1	59	27	15.93	53	31.27	79	46.61
2	1.18	28	16.52	54	31.86	80	47.20
3	1.77	29	17.11	55	32.45	81	47.79
4	2.36	30	17.70	56	33.04	82	48.38
5	2.95	31	18.29	57	33.63	83	48.97
6	3.54	32	18.88	58	34.22	84	49.56
7	4.13	33	19.47	59	34.81	85	50.15
8	4.72	34	20.06	60	35.40	86	50.74
9	5.31	35	20.65	61	35.99	87	51.33
10	5.90	36	21.24	62	36.58	88	51.92
11	6.49	37	21.83	63	37.17	89	52.51
12	7.08	38	22.42	64	37.76	90	53.10
13	7.67	39	23.01	65	38.35	91	53.69
14	8.26	40	23.60	66	38.94	92	54.28
15	8.85	41	24.19	67	39.53	93	54.87
16	9.44	42	24.78	68	40.12	94	55.46
17	10.03	43	25.37	69	40.71	95	56.05
18	10.62	44	25.96	70	41.30	96	56.64
19	11.21	45	26.55	71	41.89	97	57.23
20	11.80	46	27.14	72	42.48	98	57.82
21	12.39	47	27.73	73	43.07	99	58.41
22	12.98	48	28.32	74	43.66	100	59.00
23	13.57	49	28.91	75	44.25	200	118.00
24	14.16	50	29.50	76	44.84	400	236.00
25	14.75	51	30.09	77	45.43	600	354.00
26	15.34	52	30.68	78	46.02	1000	590.00

60 NEW PENCE

	£.np.		£.np.		£.np.		£.np.
1	60	27	16.20	53	31.80	79	47.40
2	1.20	28	16.80	54	32.40	80	48.00
3	1.80	29	17.40	55	33.00	81	48.60
4	2.40	30	18.00	56	33.60	82	49.20
5	3.00	31	18.60	57	34.20	83	49.80
6	3.60	32	19.20	58	34.80	84	50.40
7	4.20	33	19.80	59	35.40	85	51.00
8	4.80	34	20.40	60	36.00	86	51.60
9	5.40	35	21.00	61	36.60	87	52.20
10	6.00	36	21.60	62	37.20	88	52.80
11	6.60	37	22.20	63	37.80	89	53.40
12	7.20	38	22.80	64	38.40	90	54.00
13	7.80	39	23.40	65	39.00	91	54.60
14	8.40	40	24.00	66	39.60	92	55.20
15	9.00	41	24.60	67	40.20	93	55.80
16	9.60	42	25.20	68	40.80	94	56.40
17	10.20	43	25.80	69	41.40	95	57.00
18	10.80	44	26.40	70	42.00	96	57.60
19	11.40	45	27.00	71	42.60	97	58.20
20	12.00	46	27.60	72	43.20	98	58.80
21	12.60	47	28.20	73	43.80	99	59.40
22	13.20	48	28.80	74	44.40	100	60.00
23	13.80	49	29.40	75	45.00	200	120.00
24	14.40	50	30.00	76	45.60	400	240.00
25	15.00	51	30.60	77	46.20	600	360.00
26	15.60	52	31.20	78	46.80	1000	600.00

61 NEW PENCE

	£.np.		£.np.		£.np.		£.np.
1	61	27	16.47	53	32.33	79	48.19
2	1.22	28	17.08	54	32.94	80	48.80
3	1.83	29	17.69	55	33.55	81	49.41
4	2.44	30	18.30	56	34.16	82	50.02
5	3.05	31	18.91	57	34.77	83	50.63
6	3.66	32	19.52	58	35.38	84	51.24
7	4.27	33	20.13	59	35.99	85	51.85
8	4.88	34	20.74	60	36.60	86	52.46
9	5.49	35	21.35	61	37.21	87	53.07
10	6.10	36	21.96	62	37.82	88	53.68
11	6.71	37	22.57	63	38.43	89	54.29
12	7.32	38	23.18	64	39.04	90	54.90
13	7.93	39	23.79	65	39.65	91	55.51
14	8.54	40	24.40	66	40.26	92	56.12
15	9.15	41	25.01	67	40.87	93	56.73
16	9.76	42	25.62	68	41.48	94	57.34
17	10.37	43	26.23	69	42.09	95	57.95
18	10.98	44	26.84	70	42.70	96	58.56
19	11.59	45	27.45	71	43.31	97	59.17
20	12.20	46	28.06	72	43.92	98	59.78
21	12.81	47	28.67	73	44.53	99	60.39
22	13.42	48	29.28	74	45.14	100	61.00
23	14.03	49	29.89	75	45.75	200	122.00
24	14.64	50	30.50	76	46.36	400	244.00
25	15.25	51	31.11	77	46.97	600	366.00
26	15.86	52	31.72	78	47.58	1000	610.00

	£.np.		£.np.		£.np.		£.np.
1	62	27	16.74	53	32.86	79	48.98
2	1.24	28	17.36	54	33.48	80	49.60
3	1.86	29	17.98	55	34.10	81	50.22
4	2.48	30	18.60	56	34.72	82	50.84
5	3.10	31	19.22	57	35.34	83	51.46
6	3.72	32	19.84	58	35.96	84	52.08
7	4.34	33	20.46	59	36.58	85	52.70
8	4.96	34	21.08	60	37.20	86	53.32
9	5.58	35	21.70	61	37.82	87	53.94
10	6.20	36	22.32	62	38.44	88	54.56
11	6.82	37	22.94	63	39.06	89	55.18
12	7.44	38	23.56	64	39.68	90	55.80
13	8.06	39	24.18	65	40.30	91	56.42
14	8.68	40	24.80	66	40.92	92	57.04
15	9.30	41	25.42	67	41.54	93	57.66
16	9.92	42	26.04	68	42.16	94	58.28
17	10.54	43	26.66	69	42.78	95	58.90
18	11.16	44	27.28	70	43.40	96	59.52
19	11.78	45	27.90	71	44.02	97	60.14
20	12.40	46	28.52	72	44.64	98	60.76
21	13.02	47	29.14	73	45.26	99	61.38
22	13.64	48	29.76	74	45.88	100	62.00
23	14.26	49	30.38	75	46.50	200	124.00
24	14.88	50	31.00	76	47.12	400	248.00
25	15.50	51	31.62	77	47.74	600	372.00
26	16.12	52	32.24	78	48.36	1000	620.00

63 NEW PENCE

	£.np.		£.np.		£.np.		£.np.
1	63	27	17.01	53	33.39	79	49.77
2	1.26	28	17.64	54	34.02	80	50.40
3	1.89	29	18.27	55	34.65	81	51.03
4	2.52	30	18.90	56	35.28	82	51.66
5	3.15	31	19.53	57	35.91	83	52.29
6	3.78	32	20.16	58	36.54	84	52.92
7	4.41	33	20.79	59	37.17	85	53.55
8	5.04	34	21.42	60	37.80	86	54.18
9	5.67	35	22.05	61	38.43	87	54.81
10	6.30	36	22.68	62	39.06	88	55.44
11	6.93	37	23.31	63	39.69	89	56.07
12	7.56	38	23.94	64	40.32	90	56.70
13	8.19	39	24.57	65	40.95	91	57.33
14	8.82	40	25.20	66	41.58	92	57.96
15	9.45	41	25.83	67	42.21	93	58.59
16	10.08	42	26.46	68	42.84	94	59.22
17	10.71	43	27.09	69	43.47	95	59.85
18	11.34	44	27.72	70	44.10	96	60.48
19	11.97	45	28.35	71	44.73	97	61.11
20	12.60	46	28.98	72	45.36	98	61.74
21	13.23	47	29.61	73	45.99	99	62.37
22	13.86	48	30.24	74	46.62	100	63.00
23	14.49	49	30.87	75	47.25	200	126.00
24	15.12	50	31.50	76	47.88	400	252.00
25	15.75	51	32.13	77	48.51	600	378.00
26	16.38	52	32.76	78	49.14	1000	630.00

64 NEW PENCE

	£.np.		£.np.		£.np.		£.np.
1	64	27	17.28	53	33.92	79	50.56
2	1.28	28	17.92	54	34.56	80	51.20
3	1.92	29	18.56	55	35.20	81	51.84
4	2.56	30	19.20	56	35.84	82	52.48
5	3.20	31	19.84	57	36.48	83	53.12
6	3.84	32	20.48	58	37.12	84	53.76
7	4.48	33	21.12	59	37.76	85	54.40
8	5.12	34	21.76	60	38.40	86	55.04
9	5.76	35	22.40	61	39.04	87	55.68
10	6.40	36	23.04	62	39.68	88	56.32
11	7.04	37	23.68	63	40.32	89	56.96
12	7.68	38	24.32	64	40.96	90	57.60
13	8.32	39	24.96	65	41.60	91	58.24
14	8.96	40	25.60	66	42.24	92	58.88
15	9.60	41	26.24	67	42.88	93	59.52
16	10.24	42	26.88	68	43.52	94	60.16
17	10.88	43	27.52	69	44.16	95	60.80
18	11.52	44	28.16	70	44.80	96	61.44
19	12.16	45	28.80	71	45.44	97	62.08
20	12.80	46	29.44	72	46.08	98	62.72
21	13.44	47	30.08	73	46.72	99	63.36
22	14.08	48	30.72	74	47.36	100	64.00
23	14.72	49	31.36	75	48.00	200	128.00
24	15.36	50	32.00	76	48.64	400	256.00
25	16.00	51	32.64	77	49.28	600	384.00
26	16.64	52	33.28	78	49.92	1000	640.00

65 NEW PENCE

	£.np.		£.np.		£.np.		£.np.
1	65	27	17.55	53	34.45	79	51.35
2	1.30	28	18.20	54	35.10	80	52.00
3	1.95	29	18.85	55	35.75	81	52.65
4	2.60	30	19.50	56	36.40	82	53.30
5	3.25	31	20.15	57	37.05	83	53.95
6	3.90	32	20.80	58	37.70	84	54.60
7	4.55	33	21.45	59	38.35	85	55.25
8	5.20	34	22.10	60	39.00	86	55.90
9	5.85	35	22.75	61	39.65	87	56.55
10	6.50	36	23.40	62	40.30	88	57.20
11	7.15	37	24.05	63	40.95	89	57.85
12	7.80	38	24.70	64	41.60	90	58.50
13	8.45	39	25.35	65	42.25	91	59.15
14	9.10	40	26.00	66	42.90	92	59.80
15	9.75	41	26.65	67	43.55	93	60.45
16	10.40	42	27.30	68	44.20	94	61.10
17	11.05	43	27.95	69	44.85	95	61.75
18	11.70	44	28.60	70	45.50	96	62.40
19	12.35	45	29.25	71	46.15	97	63.05
20	13.00	46	29.90	72	46.80	98	63.70
21	13.65	47	30.55	73	47.45	99	64.35
22	14.30	48	31.20	74	48.10	100	65.00
23	14.95	49	31.85	75	48.75	200	130.00
24	15.60	50	32.50	76	49.40	400	260.00
25	16.25	51	33.15	77	50.05	600	390.00
26	16.90	52	33.80	78	50.70	1000	650.00

66 NEW PENCE

	£.np.		£.np.		£.np.		£.np.
1	66	27	17.82	53	34.98	79	52.14
2	1.32	28	18.48	54	35.64	80	52.80
3	1.98	29	19.14	55	36.30	81	53.46
4	2.64	30	19.80	56	36.96	82	54.12
5	3.30	31	20.46	57	37.62	83	54.78
6	3.96	32	21.12	58	38.28	84	55.44
7	4.62	33	21.78	59	38.94	85	56.10
8	5.28	34	22.44	60	39.60	86	56.76
9	5.94	35	23.10	61	40.26	87	57.42
10	6.60	36	23.76	62	40.92	88	58.08
11	7.26	37	24.42	63	41.58	89	58.74
12	7.92	38	25.08	64	42.24	90	59.40
13	8.58	39	25.74	65	42.90	91	60.06
14	9.24	40	26.40	66	43.56	92	60.72
15	9.90	41	27.06	67	44.22	93	61.38
16	10.56	42	27.72	68	44.88	94	62.04
17	11.22	43	28.38	69	45.54	95	62.70
18	11.88	44	29.04	70	46.20	96	63.36
19	12.54	45	29.70	71	46.86	97	64.02
20	13.20	46	30.36	72	47.52	98	64.68
21	13.86	47	31.02	73	48.18	99	65.34
22	14.52	48	31.68	74	48.84	100	66.00
23	15.18	49	32.34	75	49.50	200	132.00
24	15.84	50	33.00	76	50.16	400	264.00
25	16.50	51	33.66	77	50.82	600	396.00
26	17.16	52	34.32	78	51.48	1000	660.00

67 NEW PENCE

	£.np.		£.np.		£.np.		£.np.
1	67	27	18.09	53	35.51	79	52.93
2	1.34	28	18.76	54	36.18	80	53.60
3	2.01	29	19.43	55	36.85	81	54.27
4	2.68	30	20.10	56	37.52	82	54.94
5	3.35	31	20.77	57	38.19	83	55.61
6	4.02	32	21.44	58	38.86	84	56.28
7	4.69	33	22.11	59	39.53	85	56.95
8	5.36	34	22.78	60	40.20	86	57.62
9	6.03	35	23.45	61	40.87	87	58.29
10	6.70	36	24.12	62	41.54	88	58.96
11	7.37	37	24.79	63	42.21	89	59.63
12	8.04	38	25.46	64	42.88	90	60.30
13	8.71	39	26.13	65	43.55	91	60.97
14	9.38	40	26.80	66	44.22	92	61.64
15	10.05	41	27.47	67	44.89	93	62.31
16	10.72	42	28.14	68	45.56	94	62.98
17	11.39	43	28.81	69	46.23	95	63.65
18	12.06	44	29.48	70	46.90	96	64.32
19	12.73	45	30.15	71	47.57	97	64.99
20	13.40	46	30.82	72	48.24	98	65.66
21	14.07	47	31.49	73	48.91	99	66.33
22	14.74	48	32.16	74	49.58	100	67.00
23	15.41	49	32.83	75	50.25	200	134.00
24	16.08	50	33.50	76	50.92	400	268.00
25	16.75	51	34.17	77	51.59	600	402.00
26	17.42	52	34.84	78	52.26	1000	670.00

	£.np.		£.np.		£.np.		£.np.
1	68	27	18.36	53	36.04	79	53.72
2	1.36	28	19.04	54	36.72	80	54.40
3	2.04	29	19.72	55	37.40	81	55.08
4	2.72	30	20.40	56	38.08	82	55.76
5	3.40	31	21.08	57	38.76	83	56.44
6	4.08	32	21.76	58	39.44	84	57.12
7	4.76	33	22.44	59	40.12	85	57.80
8	5.44	34	23.12	60	40.80	86	58.48
9	6.12	35	23.80	61	41.48	87	59.16
10	6.80	36	24.48	62	42.16	88	59.84
11	7.48	37	25.16	63	42.84	89	60.52
12	8.16	38	25.84	64	43.52	90	61.20
13	8.84	39	26.52	65	44.20	91	61.88
14	9.52	40	27.20	66	44.88	92	62.56
15	10.20	41	27.88	67	45.56	93	63.24
16	10.88	42	28.56	68	46.24	94	63.92
17	11.56	43	29.24	69	46.92	95	64.60
18	12.24	44	29.92	70	47.60	96	65.28
19	12.92	45	30.60	71	48.28	97	65.96
20	13.60	46	31.28	72	48.96	98	66.64
21	14.28	47	31.96	73	49.64	99	67.32
22	14.96	48	32.64	74	50.32	100	68.00
23	15.64	49	33.32	75	51.00	200	136.00
24	16.32	50	34.00	76	51.68	400	272.00
25	17.00	51	34.68	77	52.36	600	408.00
26	17.68	52	35.36	78	53.04	1000	680.00

	£.np.		£.np.		£.np.		£.np.
1	69	27	18.63	53	36.57	79	54.51
2	1.38	28	19.32	54	37.26	80	55.20
3	2.07	29	20.01	55	37.95	81	55.89
4	2.76	30	20.70	56	38.64	82	56.58
5	3.45	31	21.39	57	39.33	83	57.27
6	4.14	32	22.08	58	40.02	84	57.96
7	4.83	33	22.77	59	40.71	85	58.65
8	5.52	34	23.46	60	41.40	86	59.34
9	6.21	35	24.15	61	42.09	87	60.03
10	6.90	36	24.84	62	42.78	88	60.72
11	7.59	37	25.53	63	43.47	89	61.41
12	8.28	38	26.22	64	44.16	90	62.10
13	8.97	39	26.91	65	44.85	91	62.79
14	9.66	40	27.60	66	45.54	92	63.48
15	10.35	41	28.29	67	46.23	93	64.17
16	11.04	42	28.98	68	46.92	94	64.86
17	11.73	43	29.67	69	47.61	95	65.55
18	12.42	44	30.36	70	48.30	96	66.24
19	13.11	45	31.05	71	48.99	97	66.93
20	13.80	46	31.74	72	49.68	98	67.62
21	14.49	47	32.43	73	50.37	99	68.31
22	15.18	48	33.12	74	51.06	100	69.00
23	15.87	49	33.81	75	51.75	200	138.00
24	16.56	50	34.50	76	52.44	400	276.00
25	17.25	51	35.19	77	53.13	600	414.00
26	17.94	52	35.88	78	53.82	1000	690.00

7

	£.np.		£.np.		£.np.		£.np.
1	70	27	18.90	53	37.10	79	55.30
2	1.40	28	19.60	54	37.80	80	56.00
3	2.10	29	20.30	55	38.50	81	56.70
4	2.80	30	21.00	56	39.20	82	57.40
5	3.50	31	21.70	57	39.90	83	58.10
6	4.20	32	22.40	58	40.60	84	58.80
7	4.90	33	23.10	59	41.30	85	59.50
8	5.60	34	23.80	60	42.00	86	60.20
9	6.30	35	24.50	61	42.70	87	60.90
10	7.00	36	25.20	62	43.40	88	61.60
11	7.70	37	25.90	63	44.10	89	62.30
12	8.40	38	26.60	64	44.80	90	63.00
13	9.10	39	27.30	65	45.50	91	63.70
14	9.80	40	28.00	66	46.20	92	64.40
15	10.50	41	28.70	67	46.90	93	65.10
16	11.20	42	29.40	68	47.60	94	65.80
17	11.90	43	30.10	69	48.30	95	66.50
18	12.60	44	30.80	70	49.00	96	67.20
19	13.30	45	31.50	71	49.70	97	67.90
20	14.00	46	32.20	72	50.40	98	68.60
21	14.70	47	32.90	73	51.10	99	69.30
22	15.40	48	33.60	74	51.80	100	70.00
23	16.10	49	34.30	75	52.50	200	140.00
24	16.80	50	35.00	76	53.20	400	280.00
25	17.50	51	35.70	77	53.90	600	420.00
26	18.20	52	36.40	78	54.60	1000	700.00

	£.np.		£.np.		£.np.		£.np.
1	71	27	19.17	53	37.63	79	56.09
2	1.42	28	19.88	54	38.34	80	56.80
3	2.13	29	20.59	55	39.05	81	57.51
4	2.84	30	21.30	56	39.76	82	58.22
5	3.55	31	22.01	57	40.47	83	58.93
6	4.26	32	22.72	58	41.18	84	59.64
7	4.97	33	23.43	59	41.89	85	60.35
8	5.68	34	24.14	60	42.60	86	61.06
9	6.39	35	24.85	61	43.31	87	61.77
10	7.10	36	25.56	62	44.02	88	62.48
11	7.81	37	26.27	63	44.73	89	63.19
12	8.52	38	26.98	64	45.44	90	63.90
13	9.23	39	27.69	65	46.15	91	64.61
14	9.94	40	28.40	66	46.86	92	65.32
15	10.65	41	29.11	67	47.57	93	66.03
16	11.36	42	29.82	68	48.28	94	66.74
17	12.07	43	30.53	69	48.99	95	67.45
18	12.78	44	31.24	70	49.70	96	68.16
19	13.49	45	31.95	71	50.41	97	68.87
20	14.20	46	32.66	72	51.12	98	69.58
21	14.91	47	33.37	73	51.83	99	70.29
22	15.62	48	34.08	74	52.54	100	71.00
23	16.33	49	34.79	75	53.25	200	142.00
24	17.04	50	35.50	76	53.96	400	284.00
25	17.75	51	36.21	77	54.67	600	426.00
26	18.46	52	36.92	78	55.38	1000	710.00

	£.np.		£.np.		£.np.		£.np.
1	72	27	19.44	53	38.16	79	56.88
2	1.44	28	20.16	54	38.88	80	57.60
3	2.16	29	20.88	55	39.60	81	58.32
4	2.88	30	21.60	56	40.32	82	59.04
5	3.60	31	22.32	57	41.04	83	59.76
6	4.32	32	23.04	58	41.76	84	60.48
7	5.04	33	23.76	59	42.48	85	61.20
8	5.76	34	24.48	60	43.20	86	61.92
9	6.48	35	25.20	61	43.92	87	62.64
10	7.20	36	25.92	62	44.64	88	63.36
11	7.92	37	26.64	63	45.36	89	64.08
12	8.64	38	27.36	64	46.08	90	64.80
13	9.36	39	28.08	65	46.80	91	65.52
14	10.08	40	28.80	66	47.52	92	66.24
15	10.80	41	29.52	67	48.24	93	66.96
16	11.52	42	30.24	68	48.96	94	67.68
17	12.24	43	30.96	69	49.68	95	68.40
18	12.96	44	31.68	70	50.40	96	69.12
19	13.68	45	32.40	71	51.12	97	69.84
20	14.40	46	33.12	72	51.84	98	70.56
21	15.12	47	33.84	73	52.56	99	71.28
22	15.84	48	34.56	74	53.28	100	72.00
23	16.56	49	35.28	75	54.00	200	144.00
24	17.28	50	36.00	76	54.72	400	288.00
25	18.00	51	36.72	77	55.44	600	432.00
26	18.72	52	37.44	78	56.16	1000	720.00

	£.np.		£.np.		£.np.		£.np.
1	73	27	19.71	53	38.69	79	57.67
2	1.46	28	20.44	54	39.42	80	58.40
3	2.19	29	21.17	55	40.15	81	59.13
4	2.92	30	21.90	56	40.88	82	59.86
5	3.65	31	22.63	57	41.61	83	60.59
6	4.38	32	23.36	58	42.34	84	61.32
7	5.11	33	24.09	59	43.07	85	62.05
8	5.84	34	24.82	60	43.80	86	62.78
9	6.57	35	25.55	61	44.53	87	63.51
10	7.30	36	26.28	62	45.26	88	64.24
11	8.03	37	27.01	63	45.99	89	64.97
12	8.76	38	27.74	64	46.72	90	65.70
13	9.49	39	28.47	65	47.45	91	66.43
14	10.22	40	29.20	66	48.18	92	67.16
15	10.95	41	29.93	67	48.91	93	67.89
16	11.68	42	30.66	68	49.64	94	68.62
17	12.41	43	31.39	69	50.37	95	69.35
18	13.14	44	32.12	70	51.10	96	70.08
19	13.87	45	32.85	71	51.83	97	70.81
20	14.60	46	33.58	72	52.56	98	71.54
21	15.33	47	34.31	73	53.29	99	72.27
22	16.06	48	35.04	74	54.02	100	73.00
23	16.79	49	35.77	75	54.75	200	146.00
24	17.52	50	36.50	76	55.48	400	292.00
25	18.25	51	37.23	77	56.21	600	438.00
26	18.98	52	37.96	78	56.94	1000	730.00

	£.np.		£.np.		£.np.		£.np.
1	74	27	19.98	53	39.22	79	58.46
2	1.48	28	20.72	54	39.96	80	59.20
3	2.22	29	21.46	55	40.70	81	59.94
4	2.96	30	22.20	56	41.44	82	60.68
5	3.70	31	22.94	57	42.18	83	61.42
6	4.44	32	23.68	58	42.92	84	62.16
7	5.18	33	24.42	59	43.66	85	62.90
8	5.92	34	25.16	60	44.40	86	63.64
9	6.66	35	25.90	61	45.14	87	64.38
10	7.40	36	26.64	62	45.88	88	65.12
11	8.14	37	27.38	63	46.62	89	65.86
12	8.88	38	28.12	64	47.36	90	66.60
13	9.62	39	28.86	65	48.10	91	67.34
14	10.36	40	29.60	66	48.84	92	68.08
15	11.10	41	30.34	67	49.58	93	68.82
16	11.84	42	31.08	68	50.32	94	69.56
17	12.58	43	31.82	69	51.06	95	70.30
18	13.32	44	32.56	70	51.80	96	71.04
19	14.06	45	33.30	71	52.54	97	71.78
20	14.80	46	34.04	72	53.28	98	72.52
21	15.54	47	34.78	73	54.02	99	73.26
22	16.28	48	35.52	74	54.76	100	74.00
23	17.02	49	36.26	75	55.50	200	148.00
24	17.76	50	37.00	76	56.24	400	296.00
25	18.50	51	37.74	77	56.98	600	444.00
26	19.24	52	38.48	78	57.72	1000	740.00

	£.np.		£.np.		£.np.		£.np.
1	75	27	20.25	53	39.75	79	59.25
2	1.50	28	21.00	54	40.50	80	60.00
3	2.25	29	21.75	55	41.25	81	60.75
4	3.00	30	22.50	56	42.00	82	61.50
5	3.75	31	23.25	57	42.75	83	62.25
6	4.50	32	24.00	58	43.50	84	63.00
7	5.25	33	24.75	59	44.25	85	63.75
8	6.00	34	25.50	60	45.00	86	64.50
9	6.75	35	26.25	61	45.75	87	65.25
10	7.50	36	27.00	62	46.50	88	66.00
11	8.25	37	27.75	63	47.25	89	66.75
12	9.00	38	28.50	64	48.00	90	67.50
13	9.75	39	29.25	65	48.75	91	68.25
14	10.50	40	30.00	66	49.50	92	69.00
15	11.25	41	30.75	67	50.25	93	69.75
16	12.00	42	31.50	68	51.00	94	70.50
17	12.75	43	32.25	69	51.75	95	71.25
18	13.50	44	33.00	70	52.50	96	72.00
19	14.25	45	33.75	71	53.25	97	72.75
20	15.00	46	34.50	72	54.00	98	73.50
21	15.75	47	35.25	73	54.75	99	74.25
22	16.50	48	36.00	74	55.50	100	75.00
23	17.25	49	36.75	75	56.25	200	150.00
24	18.00	50	37.50	76	57.00	400	300.00
25	18.75	51	38.25	77	57.75	600	450.00
26	19.50	52	39.00	78	58.50	1000	750.00

	£.np.		£.np.		£.np.		£.np.
1	76	27	20.52	53	40.28	79	60.04
2	1.52	28	21.28	54	41.04	80	60.80
3	2.28	29	22.04	55	41.80	81	61.56
4	3.04	30	22.80	56	42.56	82	62.32
5	3.80	31	23.56	57	43.32	83	63.08
6	4.56	32	24.32	58	44.08	84	63.84
7	5.32	33	25.08	59	44.84	85	64.60
8	6.08	34	25.84	60	45.60	86	65.36
9	6.84	35	26.60	61	46.36	87	66.12
10	7.60	36	27.36	62	47.12	88	66.88
11	8.36	37	28.12	63	47.88	89	67.64
12	9.12	38	28.88	64	48.64	90	68.40
13	9.88	39	29.64	65	49.40	91	69.16
14	10.64	40	30.40	66	50.16	92	69.92
15	11.40	41	31.16	67	50.92	93	70.68
16	12.16	42	31.92	68	51.68	94	71.44
17	12.92	43	32.68	69	52.44	95	72.20
18	13.68	44	33.44	70	53.20	96	72.96
19	14.44	45	34.20	71	53.96	97	73.72
20	15.20	46	34.96	72	54.72	98	74.48
21	15.96	47	35.72	73	55.48	99	75.24
22	16.72	48	36.48	74	56.24	100	76.00
23	17.48	49	37.24	75	57.00	200	152.00
24	18.24	50	38.00	76	57.76	400	304.00
25	19.00	51	38.76	77	58.52	600	456.00
26	19.76	52	39.52	78	59.28	1000	760.00

	£.np.		£.np.		£.np.		£.np.
1	77	27	20.79	53	40.81	79	60.83
2	1.54	28	21.56	54	41.58	80	61.60
3	2.31	29	22.33	55	42.35	81	62.37
4	3.08	30	23.10	56	43.12	82	63.14
5	3.85	31	23.87	57	43.89	83	63.91
6	4.62	32	24.64	58	44.66	84	64.68
7	5.39	33	25.41	59	45.43	85	65.45
8	6.16	34	26.18	60	46.20	86	66.22
9	6.93	35	26.95	61	46.97	87	66.99
10	7.70	36	27.72	62	47.74	88	67.76
11	8.47	37	28.49	63	48.51	89	68.53
12	9.24	38	29.26	64	49.28	90	69.30
13	10.01	39	30.03	65	50.05	91	70.07
14	10.78	40	30.80	66	50.82	92	70.84
15	11.55	41	31.57	67	51.59	93	71.61
16	12.32	42	32.34	68	52.36	94	72.38
17	13.09	43	33.11	69	53.13	95	73.15
18	13.86	44	33.88	70	53.90	96	73.92
19	14.63	45	34.65	71	54.67	97	74.69
20	15.40	46	35.42	72	55.44	98	75.46
21	16.17	47	36.19	73	56.21	99	76.23
22	16.94	48	36.96	74	56.98	100	77.00
23	17.71	49	37.73	75	57.75	200	154.00
24	18.48	50	38.50	76	58.52	400	308.00
25	19.25	51	39.27	77	59.29	600	462.00
26	20.02	52	40.04	78	60.06	1000	770.00

	£.np.		£.np.		£.np.		£.np.
1	78	27	21.06	53	41.34	79	61.62
2	1.56	28	21.84	54	42.12	80	62.40
3	2.34	29	22.62	55	42.90	81	63.18
4	3.12	30	23.40	56	43.68	82	63.96
5	3.90	31	24.18	57	44.46	83	64.74
6	4.68	32	24.96	58	45.24	84	65.52
7	5.46	33	25.74	59	46.02	85	66.30
8	6.24	34	26.52	60	46.80	86	67.08
9	7.02	35	27.30	61	47.58	87	67.86
10	7.80	36	28.08	62	48.36	88	68.64
11	8.58	37	28.86	63	49.14	89	69.42
12	9.36	38	29.64	64	49.92	90	70.20
13	10.14	39	30.42	65	50.70	91	70.98
14	10.92	40	31.20	66	51.48	92	71.76
15	11.70	41	31.98	67	52.26	93	72.54
16	12.48	42	32.76	68	53.04	94	73.32
17	13.26	43	33.54	69	53.82	95	74.10
18	14.04	44	34.32	70	54.60	96	74.88
19	14.82	45	35.10	71	55.38	97	75.66
20	15.60	46	35.88	72	56.16	98	76.44
21	16.38	47	36.66	73	56.94	99	77.22
22	17.16	48	37.44	74	57.72	100	78.00
23	17.94	49	38.22	75	58.50	200	156.00
24	18.72	50	39.00	76	59.28	400	312.00
25	19.50	51	39.78	77	60.06	600	468.00
26	20.28	52	40.56	78	60.84	1000	780.00

	£.np.		£.np.		£.np.		£.np.
1	79	27	21.33	53	41.87	79	62.41
2	1.58	28	22.12	54	42.66	80	63.20
3	2.37	29	22.91	55	43.45	81	63.99
4	3.16	30	23.70	56	44.24	82	64.78
5	3.95	31	24.49	57	45.03	83	65.57
6	4.74	32	25.28	58	45.82	84	66.36
7	5.53	33	26.07	59	46.61	85	67.15
8	6.32	34	26.86	60	47.40	86	67.94
9	7.11	35	27.65	61	48.19	87	68.73
10	7.90	36	28.44	62	48.98	88	69.52
11	8.69	37	29.23	63	49.77	89	70.31
12	9.48	38	30.02	64	50.56	90	71.10
13	10.27	39	30.81	65	51.35	91	71.89
14	11.06	40	31.60	66	52.14	92	72.68
15	11.85	41	32.39	67	52.93	93	73.47
16	12.64	42	33.18	68	53.72	94	74.26
17	13.43	43	33.97	69	54.51	95	75.05
18	14.22	44	34.76	70	55.30	96	75.84
19	15.01	45	35.55	71	56.09	97	76.63
20	15.80	46	36.34	72	56.88	98	77.42
21	16.59	47	37.13	73	57.67	99	78.21
22	17.38	48	37.92	74	58.46	100	79.00
23	18.17	49	38.71	75	59.25	200	158.00
24	18.96	50	39.50	76	60.04	400	316.00
25	19.75	51	40.29	77	60.83	600	474.00
26	20.54	52	41.08	78	61.62	1000	790.00

80 NEW PENCE

	£.np.		£.np.		£.np.		£.np.
1	80	27	21.60	53	42.40	79	63.20
2	1.60	28	22.40	54	43.20	80	64.00
3	2.40	29	23.20	55	44.00	81	64.80
4	3.20	30	24.00	56	44.80	82	65.60
5	4.00	31	24.80	57	45.60	83	66.40
6	4.80	32	25.60	58	46.40	84	67.20
7	5.60	33	26.40	59	47.20	85	68.00
8	6.40	34	27.20	60	48.00	86	68.80
9	7.20	35	28.00	61	48.80	87	69.60
10	8.00	36	28.80	62	49.60	88	70.40
11	8.80	37	29.60	63	50.40	89	71.20
12	9.60	38	30.40	64	51.20	90	72.00
13	10.40	39	31.20	65	52.00	91	72.80
14	11.20	40	32.00	66	52.80	92	73.60
15	12.00	41	32.80	67	53.60	93	74.40
16	12.80	42	33.60	68	54.40	94	75.20
17	13.60	43	34.40	69	55.20	95	76.00
18	14.40	44	35.20	70	56.00	96	76.80
19	15.20	45	36.00	71	56.80	97	77.60
20	16.00	46	36.80	72	57.60	98	78.40
21	16.80	47	37.60	73	58.40	99	79.20
22	17.60	48	38.40	74	59.20	100	80.00
23	18.40	49	39.20	75	60.00	200	160.00
24	19.20	50	40.00	76	60.80	400	320.00
25	20.00	51	40.80	77	61.60	600	480.00
26	20.80	52	41.60	78	62.40	1000	800.00

	£.np.		£.np.		£.np.		£.np.
1	81	27	21.87	53	42.93	79	63.99
2	1.62	28	22.68	54	43.74	80	64.80
3	2.43	29	23.49	55	44.55	81	65.61
4	3.24	30	24.30	56	45.36	82	66.42
5	4.05	31	25.11	57	46.17	83	67.23
6	4.86	32	25.92	58	46.98	84	68.04
7	5.67	33	26.73	59	47.79	85	68.85
8	6.48	34	27.54	60	48.60	86	69.66
9	7.29	35	28.35	61	49.41	87	70.47
10	8.10	36	29.16	62	50.22	88	71.28
11	8.91	37	29.97	63	51.03	89	72.09
12	9.72	38	30.78	64	51.84	90	72.90
13	10.53	39	31.59	65	52.65	91	73.71
14	11.34	40	32.40	66	53.46	92	74.52
15	12.15	41	33.21	67	54.27	93	75.33
16	12.96	42	34.02	68	55.08	94	76.14
17	13.77	43	34.83	69	55.89	95	76.95
18	14.58	44	35.64	70	56.70	96	77.76
19	15.39	45	36.45	71	57.51	97	78.57
20	16.20	46	37.26	72	58.32	98	79.38
21	17.01	47	38.07	73	59.13	99	80.19
22	17.82	48	38.88	74	59.94	100	81.00
23	18.63	49	39.69	75	60.75	200	162.00
24	19.44	50	40.50	76	61.56	400	324.00
25	20.25	51	41.31	77	62.37	600	486.00
26	21.06	52	42.12	78	63.18	1000	810.00

	£.np.		£.np.		£.np.		£.np.
1	82	27	22.14	53	43.46	79	64.78
2	1.64	28	22.96	54	44.28	80	65.60
3	2.46	29	23.78	55	45.10	81	66.42
4	3.28	30	24.60	56	45.92	82	67.24
5	4.10	31	25.42	57	46.74	83	68.06
6	4.92	32	26.24	58	47.56	84	68.88
7	5.74	33	27.06	59	48.38	85	69.70
8	6.56	34	27.88	60	49.20	86	70.52
9	7.38	35	28.70	61	50.02	87	71.34
10	8.20	36	29.52	62	50.84	88	72.16
11	9.02	37	30.34	63	51.66	89	72.98
12	9.84	38	31.16	64	52.48	90	73.80
13	10.66	39	31.98	65	53.30	91	74.62
14	11.48	40	32.80	66	54.12	92	75.44
15	12.30	41	33.62	67	54.94	93	76.26
16	13.12	42	34.44	68	55.76	94	77.08
17	13.94	43	35.26	69	56.58	95	77.90
18	14.76	44	36.08	70	57.40	96	78.72
19	15.58	45	36.90	71	58.22	97	79.54
20	16.40	46	37.72	72	59.04	98	80.36
21	17.22	47	38.54	73	59.86	99	81.18
22	18.04	48	39.36	74	60.68	100	82.00
23	18.86	49	40.18	75	61.50	200	164.00
24	19.68	50	41.00	76	62.32	400	328.00
25	20.50	51	41.82	77	63.14	600	492.00
26	21.32	52	42.64	78	63.96	1000	820.00

	£.np.		£.np.		£.np.		£.np.
1	83	27	22.41	53	43.99	79	65.57
2	1.66	28	23.24	54	44.82	80	66.40
3	2.49	29	24.07	55	45.65	81	67.23
4	3.32	30	24.90	56	46.48	82	68.06
5	4.15	31	25.73	57	47.31	83	68.89
6	4.98	32	26.56	58	48.14	84	69.72
7	5.81	33	27.39	59	48.97	85	70.55
8	6.64	34	28.22	60	49.80	86	71.38
9	7.47	35	29.05	61	50.63	87	72.21
10	8.30	36	29.88	62	51.46	88	73.04
11	9.13	37	30.71	63	52.29	89	73.87
12	9.96	38	31.54	64	53.12	90	74.70
13	10.79	39	32.37	65	53.95	91	75.53
14	11.62	40	33.20	66	54.78	92	76.36
15	12.45	41	34.03	67	55.61	93	77.19
16	13.28	42	34.86	68	56.44	94	78.02
17	14.11	43	35.69	69	57.27	95	78.85
18	14.94	44	36.52	70	58.10	96	79.68
19	15.77	45	37.35	71	58.93	97	80.51
20	16.60	46	38.18	72	59.76	98	81.34
21	17.43	47	39.01	73	60.59	99	82.17
22	18.26	48	39.84	74	61.42	100	83.00
23	19.09	49	40.67	75	62.25	200	166.00
24	19.92	50	41.50	76	63.08	400	332.00
25	20.75	51	42.33	77	63.91	600	498.00
26	21.58	52	43.16	78	64.74	1000	830.00

	£.np.		£.np.		£.np.		£.np.
1	84	27	22.68	53	44.52	79	66.36
2	1.68	28	23.52	54	45.36	80	67.20
3	2.52	29	24.36	55	46.20	81	68.04
4	3.36	30	25.20	56	47.04	82	68.88
5	4.20	31	26.04	57	47.88	83	69.72
6	5.04	32	26.88	58	48.72	84	70.56
7	5.88	33	27.72	59	49.56	85	71.40
8	6.72	34	28.56	60	50.40	86	72.24
9	7.56	35	29.40	61	51.24	87	73.08
10	8.40	36	30.24	62	52.08	88	73.92
11	9.24	37	31.08	63	52.92	89	74.76
12	10.08	38	31.92	64	53.76	90	75.60
13	10.92	39	32.76	65	54.60	91	76.44
14	11.76	40	33.60	66	55.44	92	77.28
15	12.60	41	34.44	67	56.28	93	78.12
16	13.44	42	35.28	68	57.12	94	78.96
17	14.28	43	36.12	69	57.96	95	79.80
18	15.12	44	36.96	70	58.80	96	80.64
19	15.96	45	37.80	71	59.64	97	81.48
20	16.80	46	38.64	72	60.48	98	82.32
21	17.64	47	39.48	73	61.32	99	83.16
22	18.48	48	40.32	74	62.16	100	84.00
23	19.32	49	41.16	75	63.00	200	168.00
24	20.16	50	42.00	76	63.84	400	336.00
25	21.00	51	42.84	77	64.68	600	504.00
26	21.84	52	43.68	78	65.52	1000	840.00

	£.np.		£.np.		£.np.		£.np.
1	85	27	22.95	53	45.05	79	67.15
2	1.70	28	23.80	54	45.90	80	68.00
3	2.55	29	24.65	55	46.75	81	68.85
4	3.40	30	25.50	56	47.60	82	69.70
5	4.25	31	26.35	57	48.45	83	70.55
6	5.10	32	27.20	58	49.30	84	71.40
7	5.95	33	28.05	59	50.15	85	72.25
8	6.80	34	28.90	60	51.00	86	73.10
9	7.65	35	29.75	61	51.85	87	73.95
10	8.50	36	30.60	62	52.70	88	74.80
11	9.35	37	31.45	63	53.55	89	75.65
12	10.20	38	32.30	64	54.40	90	76.50
13	11.05	39	33.15	65	55.25	91	77.35
14	11.90	40	34.00	66	56.10	92	78.20
15	12.75	41	34.85	67	56.95	93	79.05
16	13.60	42	35.70	68	57.80	94	79.90
17	14.45	43	36.55	69	58.65	95	80.75
18	15.30	44	37.40	70	59.50	96	81.60
19	16.15	45	38.25	71	60.35	97	82.45
20	17.00	46	39.10	72	61.20	98	83.30
21	17.85	47	39.95	73	62.05	99	84.15
22	18.70	48	40.80	74	62.90	100	85.00
23	19.55	49	41.65	75	63.75	200	170.00
24	20.40	50	42.50	76	64.60	400	340.00
25	21.25	51	43.35	77	65.45	600	510.00
26	22.10	52	44.20	78	66.30	1000	850.00

	£.np.		£.np.		£.np.		£.np.
1	86	27	23.22	53	45.58	79	67.94
2	1.72	28	24.08	54	46.44	80	68.80
3	2.58	29	24.94	55	47.30	81	69.66
4	3.44	30	25.80	56	48.16	82	70.52
5	4.30	31	26.66	57	49.02	83	71.38
6	5.16	32	27.52	58	49.88	84	72.24
7	6.02	33	28.38	59	50.74	85	73.10
8	6.88	34	29.24	60	51.60	86	73.96
9	7.74	35	30.10	61	52.46	87	74.82
10	8.60	36	30.96	62	53.32	88	75.68
11	9.46	37	31.82	63	54.18	89	76.54
12	10.32	38	32.68	64	55.04	90	77.40
13	11.18	39	33.54	65	55.90	91	78.26
14	12.04	40	34.40	66	56.76	92	79.12
15	12.90	41	35.26	67	57.62	93	79.98
16	13.76	42	36.12	68	58.48	94	80.84
17	14.62	43	36.98	69	59.34	95	81.70
18	15.48	44	37.84	70	60.20	96	82.56
19	16.34	45	38.70	71	61.06	97	83.42
20	17.20	46	39.56	72	61.92	98	84.28
21	18.06	47	40.42	73	62.78	99	85.14
22	18.92	48	41.28	74	63.64	100	86.00
23	19.78	49	42.14	75	64.50	200	172.00
24	20.64	50	43.00	76	65.36	400	344.00
25	21.50	51	43.86	77	66.22	600	516.00
26	22.36	52	44.72	78	67.08	1000	860.00

	£.np.		£.np.		£.np.		£.np.
1	87	27	23.49	53	46.11	79	68.73
2	1.74	28	24.36	54	46.98	80	69.60
3	2.61	29	25.23	55	47.85	81	70.47
4	3.48	30	26.10	56	48.72	82	71.34
5	4.35	31	26.97	57	49.59	83	72.21
6	5.22	32	27.84	58	50.46	84	73.08
7	6.09	33	28.71	59	51.33	85	73.95
8	6.96	34	29.58	60	52.20	86	74.82
9	7.83	35	30.45	61	53.07	87	75.69
10	8.70	36	31.32	62	53.94	88	76.56
11	9.57	37	32.19	63	54.81	89	77.43
12	10.44	38	33.06	64	55.68	90	78.30
13	11.31	39	33.93	65	56.55	91	79.17
14	12.18	40	34.80	66	57.42	92	80.04
15	13.05	41	35.67	67	58.29	93	80.91
16	13.92	42	36.54	68	59.16	94	81.78
17	14.79	43	37.41	69	60.03	95	82.65
18	15.66	44	38.28	70	60.90	96	83.52
19	16.53	45	39.15	71	61.77	97	84.39
20	17.40	46	40.02	72	62.64	98	85.26
21	18.27	47	40.89	73	63.51	99	86.13
22	19.14	48	41.76	74	64.38	100	87.00
23	20.01	49	42.63	75	65.25	200	174.00
24	20.88	50	43.50	76	66.12	400	348.00
25	21.75	51	44.37	77	66.99	600	522.00
26	22.62	52	45.24	78	67.86	1000	870.00

	£.np.		£.np.		£.np.		£.np.
1	88	27	23.76	53	46.64	79	69.52
2	1.76	28	24.64	54	47.52	80	70.40
3	2.64	29	25.52	55	48.40	81	71.28
4	3.52	30	26.40	56	49.28	82	72.16
5	4.40	31	27.28	57	50.16	83	73.04
6	5.28	32	28.16	58	51.04	84	73.92
7	6.16	33	29.04	59	51.92	85	74.80
8	7.04	34	29.92	60	52.80	86	75.68
9	7.92	35	30.80	61	53.68	87	76.56
10	8.80	36	31.68	62	54.56	88	77.44
11	9.68	37	32.56	63	55.44	89	78.32
12	10.56	38	33.44	64	56.32	90	79.20
13	11.44	39	34.32	65	57.20	91	80.08
14	12.32	40	35.20	66	58.08	92	80.96
15	13.20	41	36.08	67	58.96	93	81.84
16	14.08	42	36.96	68	59.84	94	82.72
17	14.96	43	37.84	69	60.72	95	83.60
18	15.84	44	38.72	70	61.60	96	84.48
19	16.72	45	39.60	71	62.48	97	85.36
20	17.60	46	40.48	72	63.36	98	86.24
21	18.48	47	41.36	73	64.24	99	87.12
22	19.36	48	42.24	74	65.12	100	88.00
23	20.24	49	43.12	75	66.00	200	176.00
24	21.12	50	44.00	76	66.88	400	352.00
25	22.00	51	44.88	77	67.76	600	528.00
26	22.88	52	45.76	78	68.64	1000	880.00

	£.np.		£.np.		£.np.		£.np.
1	89	27	24.03	53	47.17	79	70.31
2	1.78	28	24.92	54	48.06	80	71.20
3	2.67	29	25.81	55	48.95	81	72.09
4	3.56	30	26.70	56	49.84	82	72.98
5	4.45	31	27.59	57	50.73	83	73.87
6	5.34	32	28.48	58	51.62	84	74.76
7	6.23	33	29.37	59	52.51	85	75.65
8	7.12	34	30.26	60	53.40	86	76.54
9	8.01	35	31.15	61	54.29	87	77.43
10	8.90	36	32.04	62	55.18	88	78.32
11	9.79	37	32.93	63	56.07	89	79.21
12	10.68	38	33.82	64	56.96	90	80.10
13	11.57	39	34.71	65	57.85	91	80.99
14	12.46	40	35.60	66	58.74	92	81.88
15	13.35	41	36.49	67	59.63	93	82.77
16	14.24	42	37.38	68	60.52	94	83.66
17	15.13	43	38.27	69	61.41	95	84.55
18	16.02	44	39.16	70	62.30	96	85.44
19	16.91	45	40.05	71	63.19	97	86.33
20	17.80	46	40.94	72	64.08	98	87.22
21	18.69	47	41.83	73	64.97	99	88.11
22	19.58	48	42.72	74	65.86	100	89.00
23	20.47	49	43.61	75	66.75	200	178.00
24	21.36	50	44.50	76	67.64	400	356.00
25	22.25	51	45.39	77	68.53	600	534.00
26	23.14	52	46.28	78	69.42	1000	890.00

90 NEW PENCE

	£.np.		£.np.		£.np.		£.np.
1	90	27	24.30	53	47.70	79	71.10
2	1.80	28	25.20	54	48.60	80	72.00
3	2.70	29	26.10	55	49.50	81	72.90
4	3.60	30	27.00	56	50.40	82	73.80
5	4.50	31	27.90	57	51.30	83	74.70
6	5.40	32	28.80	58	52.20	84	75.60
7	6.30	33	29.70	59	53.10	85	76.50
8	7.20	34	30.60	60	54.00	86	77.40
9	8.10	35	31.50	61	54.90	87	78.30
10	9.00	36	32.40	62	55.80	88	79.20
11	9.90	37	33.30	63	56.70	89	80.10
12	10.80	38	34.20	64	57.60	90	81.00
13	11.70	39	35.10	65	58.50	91	81.90
14	12.60	40	36.00	66	59.40	92	82.80
15	13.50	41	36.90	67	60.30	93	83.70
16	14.40	42	37.80	68	61.20	94	84.60
17	15.30	43	38.70	69	62.10	95	85.50
18	16.20	44	39.60	70	63.00	96	86.40
19	17.10	45	40.50	71	63.90	97	87.30
20	18.00	46	41.40	72	64.80	98	88.20
21	18.90	47	42.30	73	65.70	99	89.10
22	19.80	48	43.20	74	66.60	100	90.00
23	20.70	49	44.10	75	67.50	200	180.00
24	21.60	50	45.00	76	68.40	400	360.00
25	22.50	51	45.90	77	69.30	600	540.00
26	23.40	52	46.80	78	70.20	1000	900.00

	£.np.		£.np.		£.np.		£.np.
1	91	27	24.57	53	48.23	79	71.89
2	1.82	28	25.48	54	49.14	80	72.80
3	2.73	29	26.39	55	50.05	81	73.71
4	3.64	30	27.30	56	50.96	82	74.62
5	4.55	31	28.21	57	51.87	83	75.53
6	5.46	32	29.12	58	52.78	84	76.44
7	6.37	33	30.03	59	53.69	85	77.35
8	7.28	34	30.94	60	54.60	86	78.26
9	8.19	35	31.85	61	55.51	87	79.17
10	9.10	36	32.76	62	56.42	88	80.08
11	10.01	37	33.67	63	57.33	89	80.99
12	10.92	38	34.58	64	58.24	90	81.90
13	11.83	39	35.49	65	59.15	91	82.81
14	12.74	40	36.40	66	60.06	92	83.72
15	13.65	41	37.31	67	60.97	93	84.63
16	14.56	42	38.22	68	61.88	94	85.54
17	15.47	43	39.13	69	62.79	95	86.45
18	16.38	44	40.04	70	63.70	96	87.36
19	17.29	45	40.95	71	64.61	97	88.27
20	18.20	46	41.86	72	65.52	98	89.18
21	19.11	47	42.77	73	66.43	99	90.09
22	20.02	48	43.68	74	67.34	100	91.00
23	20.93	49	44.59	75	68.25	200	182.00
24	21.84	50	45.50	76	69.16	400	364.00
25	22.75	51	46.41	77	70.07	600	546.00
26	23.66	52	47.32	78	70.98	1000	910.00

	£.np.		£.np.		£.np.		£.np.
1	92	27	24.84	53	48.76	79	72.68
2	1.84	28	25.76	54	49.68	80	73.60
3	2.76	29	26.68	55	50.60	81	74.52
4	3.68	30	27.60	56	51.52	82	75.44
5	4.60	31	28.52	57	52.44	83	76.36
6	5.52	32	29.44	58	53.36	84	77.28
7	6.44	33	30.36	59	54.28	85	78.20
8	7.36	34	31.28	60	55.20	86	79.12
9	8.28	35	32.20	61	56.12	87	80.04
10	9.20	36	33.12	62	57.04	88	80.96
11	10.12	37	34.04	63	57.96	89	81.88
12	11.04	38	34.96	64	58.88	90	82.80
13	11.96	39	35.88	65	59.80	91	83.72
14	12.88	40	36.80	66	60.72	92	84.64
15	13.80	41	37.72	67	61.64	93	85.56
16	14.72	42	38.64	68	62.56	94	86.48
17	15.64	43	39.56	69	63.48	95	87.40
18	16.56	44	40.48	70	64.40	96	88.32
19	17.48	45	41.40	71	65.32	97	89.24
20	18.40	46	42.32	72	66.24	98	90.16
21	19.32	47	43.24	73	67.16	99	91.08
22	20.24	48	44.16	74	68.08	100	92.00
23	21.16	49	45.08	75	69.00	200	184.00
24	22.08	50	46.00	76	69.92	400	368.00
25	23.00	51	46.92	77	70.84	600	552.00
26	23.92	52	47.84	78	71.76	1000	920.00

	£.np.		£.np.		£.np.		£.np.
1	93	27	25.11	53	49.29	79	73.47
2	1.86	28	26.04	54	50.22	80	74.40
3	2.79	29	26.97	55	51.15	81	75.33
4	3.72	30	27.90	56	52.08	82	76.26
5	4.65	31	28.83	57	53.01	83	77.19
6	5.58	32	29.76	58	53.94	84	78.12
7	6.51	33	30.69	59	54.87	85	79.05
8	7.44	34	31.62	60	55.80	86	79.98
9	8.37	35	32.55	61	56.73	87	80.91
10	9.30	36	33.48	62	57.66	88	81.84
11	10.23	37	34.41	63	58.59	89	82.77
12	11.16	38	35.34	64	59.52	90	83.70
13	12.09	39	36.27	65	60.45	91	84.63
14	13.02	40	37.20	66	61.38	92	85.56
15	13.95	41	38.13	67	62.31	93	86.49
16	14.88	42	39.06	68	63.24	94	87.42
17	15.81	43	39.99	69	64.17	95	88.35
18	16.74	44	40.92	70	65.10	96	89.28
19	17.67	45	41.85	71	66.03	97	90.21
20	18.60	46	42.78	72	66.96	98	91.14
21	19.53	47	43.71	73	67.89	99	92.07
22	20.46	48	44.64	74	68.82	100	93.00
23	21.39	49	45.57	75	69.75	200	186.00
24	22.32	50	46.50	76	70.68	400	372.00
25	23.25	51	47.43	77	71.61	600	558.00
26	24.18	52	48.36	78	72.54	1000	930.00

	£.np.		£.np.		£.np.		£.np.
1	94	27	25.38	53	49.82	79	74.26
2	1.88	28	26.32	54	50.76	80	75.20
3	2.82	29	27.26	55	51.70	81	76.14
4	3.76	30	28.20	56	52.64	82	77.08
5	4.70	31	29.14	57	53.58	83	78.02
6	5.64	32	30.08	58	54.52	84	78.96
7	6.58	33	31.02	59	55.46	85	79.90
8	7.52	34	31.96	60	56.40	86	80.84
9	8.46	35	32.90	61	57.34	87	81.78
10	9.40	36	33.84	62	58.28	88	82.72
11	10.34	37	34.78	63	59.22	89	83.66
12	11.28	38	35.72	64	60.16	90	84.60
13	12.22	39	36.66	65	61.10	91	85.54
14	13.16	40	37.60	66	62.04	92	86.48
15	14.10	41	38.54	67	62.98	93	87.42
16	15.04	42	39.48	68	63.92	94	88.36
17	15.98	43	40.42	69	64.86	95	89.30
18	16.92	44	41.36	70	65.80	96	90.24
19	17.86	45	42.30	71	66.74	97	91.18
20	18.80	46	43.24	72	67.68	98	92.12
21	19.74	47	44.18	73	68.62	99	93.06
22	20.68	48	45.12	74	69.56	100	94.00
23	21.62	49	46.06	75	70.50	200	188.00
24	22.56	50	47.00	76	71.44	400	376.00
25	23.50	51	47.94	77	72.38	600	564.00
26	24.44	52	48.88	78	73.32	1000	940.00

	£.np.		£.np.		£.np.		£.np.
1	95	27	25.65	53	50.35	79	75.05
2	1.90	28	26.60	54	51.30	80	76.00
3	2.85	29	27.55	55	52.25	81	76.95
4	3.80	30	28.50	56	53.20	82	77.90
5	4.75	31	29.45	57	54.15	83	78.85
6	5.70	32	30.40	58	55.10	84	79.80
7	6.65	33	31.35	59	56.05	85	80.75
8	.7.60	34	32.30	60	57.00	86	81.70
9	8.55	35	33.25	61	57.95	87	82.65
10	9.50	36	34.20	62	58.90	88	83.60
11	10.45	37	35.15	63	59.85	89	84.55
12	11.40	38	36.10	64	60.80	90	85.50
13	12.35	39	37.05	65	61.75	91	86.45
14	13.30	40	38.00	66	62.70	92	87.40
15	14.25	41	38.95	67	63.65	93	88.35
16	15.20	42	39.90	68	64.60	94	89.30
17	16.15	43	40.85	69	65.55	95	90.25
18	17.10	44	41.80	70	66.50	96	91.20
19	18.05	45	42.75	71	67.45	97	92.15
20	19.00	46	43.70	72	68.40	98	93.10
21	19.95	47	44.65	73	69.35	99	94.05
22	20.90	48	45.60	74	70.30	100	95.00
23	21.85	49	46.55	75	71.25	200	190.00
24	22.80	50	47.50	76	72.20	400	380.00
25	23.75	51	48.45	77	73.15	600	570.00
26	24.70	52	49.40	78	74.10	1000	950.00

	£.np.		£.np.		£.np.		£.np.
1	96	27	25.92	53	50.88	79	75.84
2	1.92	28	26.88	54	51.84	80	76.80
3	2.88	29	27.84	55	52.80	81	77.76
4	3.84	30	28.80	56	53.76	82	78.72
5	4.80	31	29.76	57	54.72	83	79.68
6	5.76	32	30.72	58	55.68	84	80.64
7	6.72	33	31.68	59	56.64	85	81.60
8	7.68	34	32.64	60	57.60	86	82.56
9	8.64	35	33.60	61	58.56	87	83.52
10	9.60	36	34.56	62	59.52	88	84.48
11	10.56	37	35.52	63	60.48	89	85.44
12	11.52	38	36.48	64	61.44	90	86.40
13	12.48	39	37.44	65	62.40	91	87.36
14	13.44	40	38.40	66	63.36	92	88.32
15	14.40	41	39.36	67	64.32	93	89.28
16	15.36	42	40.32	68	65.28	94	90.24
17	16.32	43	41.28	69	66.24	95	91.20
18	17.28	44	42.24	70	67.20	96	92.16
19	18.24	45	43.20	71	68.16	97	93.12
20	19.20	46	44.16	72	69.12	98	94.08
21	20.16	47	45.12	73	70.08	99	95.04
22	21.12	48	46.08	74	71.04	100	96.00
23	22.08	49	47.04	75	72.00	200	192.00
24	23.04	50	48.00	76	72.96	400	384.00
25	24.00	51	48.96	77	73.92	600	576.00
26	24.96	52	49.92	78	74.88	1000	960.00

	£.np.		£.np.		£.np.		£.np.
1	97	27	26.19	53	51.41	79	76.63
2	1.94	28	27.16	54	52.38	80	77.60
3	2.91	29	28.13	55	53.35	81	78.57
4	3.88	30	29.10	56	54.32	82	79.54
5	4.85	31	30.07	57	55.29	83	80.51
6	5.82	32	31.04	58	56.26	84	81.48
7	6.79	33	32.01	59	57.23	85	82.45
8	7.76	34	32.98	60	58.20	86	83.42
9	8.73	35	33.95	61	59.17	87	84.39
10	9.70	36	34.92	62	60.14	88	85.36
11	10.67	37	35.89	63	61.11	89	86.33
12	11.64	38	36.86	64	62.08	90	87.30
13	12.61	39	37.83	65	63.05	91	88.27
14	13.58	40	38.80	66	64.02	92	89.24
15	14.55	41	39.77	67	64.99	93	90.21
16	15.52	42	40.74	68	65.96	94	91.18
17	16.49	43	41.71	69	66.93	95	92.15
18	17.46	44	42.68	70	67.90	96	93.12
19	18.43	45	43.65	71	68.87	97	94.09
20	19.40	46	44.62	72	69.84	98	95.06
21	20.37	47	45.59	73	70.81	99	96.03
22	21.34	48	46.56	74	71.78	100	97.00
23	22.31	49	47.53	75	72.75	200	194.00
24	23.28	50	48.50	76	73.72	400	388.00
25	24.25	51	49.47	77	74.69	600	582.00
26	25.22	52	50.44	78	75.66	1000	970.00

	£.np.		£.np.		£.np.		£.np.
1	98	27	26.46	53	51.94	79	77.42
2	1.96	28	27.44	54	52.92	80	78.40
3	2.94	29	28.42	55	53.90	81	79.38
4	3.92	30	29.40	56	54.88	82	80.36
5	4.90	31	30.38	57	55.86	83	81.34
6	5.88	32	31.36	58	56.84	84	82.32
7	6.86	33	32.34	59	57.82	85	83.30
8	7.84	34	33.32	60	58.80	86	84.28
9	8.82	35	34.30	61	59.78	87	85.26
10	9.80	36	35.28	62	60.76	88	86.24
11	10.78	37	36.26	63	61.74	89	87.22
12	11.76	38	37.24	64	62.72	90	88.20
13	12.74	39	38.22	65	63.70	91	89.18
14	13.72	40	39.20	66	64.68	92	90.16
15	14.70	41	40.18	67	65.66	93	91.14
16	15.68	42	41.16	68	66.64	94	92.12
17	16.66	43	42.14	69	67.62	95	93.10
18	17.64	44	43.12	70	68.60	96	94.08
19	18.62	45	44.10	71	69.58	97	95.06
20	19.60	46	45.08	72	70.56	98	96.04
21	20.58	47	46.06	73	71.54	99	97.02
22	21.56	48	47.04	74	72.52	100	98.00
23	22.54	49	48.02	75	73.50	200	196.00
24	23.52	50	49.00	76	74.48	400	392.00
25	24.50	51	49.98	77	75.46	600	588.00
26	25.48	52	50.96	78	76.44	1000	980.00

	£.np.		£.np.		£.np.		£.np.
1	99	27	26.73	53	52.47	79	78.21
2	1.98	28	27.72	54	53.46	80	79.20
3	2.97	29	28.71	55	54.45	81	80.19
4	3.96	30	29.70	56	55.44	82	81.18
5	4.95	31	30.69	57	56.43	83	82.17
6	5.94	32	31.68	58	57.42	84	83.16
7	6.93	33	32.67	59	58.41	85	84.15
8	7.92	34	33.66	60	59.40	86	85.14
9	8.91	35	34.65	61	60.39	87	86.13
10	9.90	36	35.64	62	61.38	88	87.12
11	10.89	37	36.63	63	62.37	89	88.11
12	11.88	38	37.62	64	63.36	90	89.10
13	12.87	39	38.61	65	64.35	91	90.09
14	13.86	40	39.60	66	65.34	92	91.08
15	14.85	41	40.59	67	66.33	93	92.07
16	15.84	42	41.58	68	67.32	94	93.06
17	16.83	43	42.57	69	68.31	95	94.05
18	17.82	44	43.56	70	69.30	96	95.04
19	18.81	45	44.55	71	70.29	97	96.03
20	19.80	46	45.54	72	71.28	98	97.02
21	20.79	47	46.53	73	72.27	99	98.01
22	21.78	48	47.52	74	73.26	100	99.00
23	22.77	49	48.51	75	74.25	200	198.00
24	23.76	50	49.50	76	75.24	400	396.00
25	24.75	51	50.49	77	76.23	600	594.00
26	25.74	52	51.48	78	77.22	1000	990.00

LENGTH CONVERSION TABLE
INCHES TO CENTIMETRES

In.	Cm.	In.	Cm.	In.	Cm.	In.	Cm.
1	2.540	27	68.580	53	134.620	79	200.660
2	5.080	28	71.120	54	137.160	80	203.200
3	7.620	29	73.660	55	139,700	81	205.740
4	10.160	30	76.200	56	142.240	82	208.280
5	12.700	31	78.740	57	144.780	83	210.820
6	15.240	32	81.280	58	147.320	84	213.360
7	17.780	33	83.820	59	149.860	85	215.900
8	20.320	34	86.360	60	152.400	86	218.440
9	22.860	35	88.900	61	154.940	87	220.980
10	25.400	36	91.440	62	157.480	88	223.520
11	27.940	37	93.980	63	160.020	89	226.060
12	30.480	38	96.520	64	162.560	90	228.600
13	33.020	39	99.060	65	165.100	91	231.140
14	35.560	40	101.600	66	167.640	92	233.680
15	38.100	41	104.140	67	170.180	93	236.220
16	40.640	42	106.680	68	172.720	94	238.760
17	43.180	43	109.220	69	175.260	95	241.300
18	45.720	44	111.760	70	177.800	96	243.840
19	48.260	45	114.300	71	180.340	97	246.380
20	50.800	46	116.840	72	182.880	98	248.920
21	53.340	47	119.380	73	185.420	99	251.460
22	55.880	48	121.920	74	187.960	100	254.000
23	58.420	49	124.460	75	190.500	200	508.000
24	60.960	50	127.000	76	193.040	400	1016.000
25	63.500	51	129.540	77	195.580	600	1524.000
26	66.040	52	132.080	78	198.120	1000	2540.000

To obtain millimetre readings move the decimal point one place
to the right, e.g. 1″ = 25.40 millimetres.

LENGTH CONVERSION TABLE
CENTIMETRES TO INCHES

Cm.	In.	Cm.	In.	Cm.	In.	Cm.	In.
1	0.394	27	10.630	53	20.867	79	31.103
2	0.787	28	11.024	54	21.260	80	31.496
3	1.181	29	11.418	55	21.654	81	31.890
4	1.575	30	11.811	56	22.048	82	32.283
5	1.969	31	12.205	57	22.441	83	32.677
6	2.362	32	12.598	58	22.835	84	33.071
7	2.756	33	12.992	59	23.229	85	33.465
8	3.150	34	13.386	60	23.622	86	33.859
9	3.543	35	13.780	61	24.016	87	34.253
10	3.937	36	14.173	62	24.409	88	34.646
11	4.331	37	14.567	63	24.803	89	35.040
12	4.724	38	14.961	64	25.197	90	35.433
13	5.118	39	15.355	65	25.591	91	35.827
14	5.512	40	15.748	66	25.985	92	36.220
15	5.906	41	16.142	67	26.378	93	36.614
16	6.299	42	16.535	68	26.772	94	37.008
17	6.693	43	16.929	69	27.166	95	37.402
18	7.087	44	17.323	70	27.559	96	37.796
19	7.481	45	17.717	71	27.953	97	38.189
20	7.874	46	18.110	72	28.346	98	38.583
21	8.268	47	18.504	73	28.740	99	38.977
22	8.661	48	18.898	74	29.134	100	39.370
23	9.055	49	19.292	75	29.528	200	78.740
24	9.449	50	19.685	76	29.922	400	157.480
25	9.843	51	20.079	77	30.315	600	236.220
26	10.236	52	20.473	78	30.709	1000	393.700

To obtain millimetre readings move the decimal point one place to the left. e.g. 1 millimetre = 0.0394 inches

9

LENGTH CONVERSION TABLE
YARDS TO METRES

Yd.	M.	Yd.	M.	Yd.	M.	Yd.	M.
1	0.914	27	24.688	53	48.463	79	72.238
2	1.829	28	25.603	54	49.378	80	73.152
3	2.743	29	26.517	55	50.292	81	74.066
4	3.658	30	27.432	56	51.206	82	74.981
5	4.572	31	28.346	57	52.121	83	75.895
6	5.486	32	29.261	58	53.035	84	76.810
7	6.401	33	30.175	59	53.949	85	77.724
8	7.315	34	31.090	60	54.864	86	78.638
9	8.230	35	32.004	61	55.778	87	79.553
10	9.144	36	32.918	62	56.693	88	80.467
11	10.058	37	33.832	63	57.607	89	81.382
12	10.973	38	34.747	64	58.522	90	82.296
13	11.887	39	35.661	65	59.436	91	83.210
14	12.802	40	36.576	66	60.350	92	84.125
15	13.716	41	37.490	67	61.265	93	85.039
16	14.630	42	38.405	68	62.179	94	85.954
17	15.544	43	39.319	69	63.094	95	86.868
18	16.459	44	40.234	70	64.008	96	87.782
19	17.373	45	41.148	71	64.922	97	88.697
20	18.288	46	42.062	72	65.837	98	89.611
21	19.203	47	42.976	73	66.751	99	90.526
22	20.117	48	43.891	74	67.666	100	91.440
23	21.032	49	44.805	75	68.580	200	182.880
24	21.946	50	45.720	76	69.494	400	365.760
25	22.860	51	46.634	77	70.409	600	548.640
26	23.774	52	47.549	78	71.323	1000	914.400

LENGTH CONVERSION TABLE
METRES TO YARDS

M.	Yd.	M.	Yd.	M.	Yd.	M.	Yd.
1	1.094	27	29.528	53	57.962	79	86.395
2	2.187	28	30.621	54	59.055	80	87.489
3	3.281	29	31.715	55	60.149	81	88.583
4	4.374	30	32.808	56	61.243	82	89.676
5	5.468	31	33.902	57	62.336	83	90.770
6	6.562	32	34.996	58	63.430	84	91.863
7	7.655	33	36.090	59	64.523	85	92.957
8	8.749	34	37.183	60	65.617	86	94.051
9	9.843	35	38.277	61	66.711	87	95.144
10	10.936	36	39.370	62	67.804	88	96.238
11	12.030	37	40.464	63	68.898	89	97.331
12	13.123	38	41.557	64	69.991	90	98.425
13	14.217	39	42.651	65	71.085	91	99.519
14	15.311	40	43.745	66	72.179	92	100.612
15	16.405	41	44.839	67	73.272	93	101.706
16	17.498	42	45.932	68	74.366	94	102.799
17	18.592	43	47.026	69	75.459	95	103.893
18	19.685	44	48.119	70	76.553	96	104.987
19	20.779	45	49.213	71	77.647	97	106.080
20	21.872	46	50.306	72	78.740	98	107.174
21	22.966	47	51.400	73	79.834	99	108.267
22	24.059	48	52.493	74	80.927	100	109.361
23	25.153	49	53.587	75	82.021	200	218.722
24	26.247	50	54.681	76	83.115	400	437.444
25	27.341	51	55.775	77	84.208	600	656.166
26	28.434	52	56.868	78	85.302	1000	1093.610

AREA CONVERSION TABLE
SQUARE YARDS TO SQUARE METRES

Sq.yd.	Sq.m.	Sq.yd.	Sq.m.	Sq.yd.	Sq.m.	Sq.yd.	Sq.m.
1	0.836	27	22.575	53	44.315	79	66.054
2	1.672	28	23.412	54	45.151	80	66.890
3	2.508	29	24.248	55	45.987	81	67.726
4	3.345	30	25.084	56	46.823	82	68.562
5	4.181	31	25.920	57	47.659	83	69.398
6	5.017	32	26.756	58	48.495	84	70.235
7	5.853	33	27.592	59	49.332	85	71.071
8	6.689	34	28.428	60	50.168	86	71.907
9	7.525	35	29.264	61	51.004	87	72.743
10	8.361	36	30.101	62	51.840	88	73.579
11	9.197	37	30.937	63	52.676	89	74.416
12	10.034	38	31.773	64	53.512	90	75.252
13	10.870	39	32.609	65	54.348	91	76.088
14	11.706	40	33.445	66	55.184	92	76.924
15	12.542	41	34.281	67	56.020	93	77.760
16	13.378	42	35.117	68	56.856	94	78.597
17	14.214	43	35.953	69	57.693	95	79.432
18	15.050	44	36.790	70	58.529	96	80.268
19	15.886	45	37.626	71	59.365	97	81.104
20	16.723	46	38.462	72	60.201	98	81.940
21	17.559	47	39.298	73	61.037	99	82.777
22	18.395	48	40.134	74	61.874	100	83.613
23	19.231	49	40.970	75	62.710	200	167.226
24	20.067	50	41.807	76	63.546	400	334.452
25	20.903	51	42.643	77	64.382	600	501.678
26	21.739	52	43.479	78	65.218	1000	836.130

AREA CONVERSION TABLE
SQUARE METRES TO SQUARE YARDS

Sq.m.	Sq.yd.	Sq.m.	Sq.yd.	Sq.m.	Sq.yd.	Sq.m.	Sq.yd.
1	1.196	27	32.292	53	63.388	79	94.484
2	2.392	28	33.488	54	64.584	80	95.680
3	3.588	29	34.684	55	65.780	81	96.876
4	4.784	30	35.880	56	66.976	82	98.072
5	5.980	31	37.076	57	68.172	83	99.268
6	7.176	32	38.272	58	69.368	84	100.464
7	8.372	33	39.468	59	70.564	85	101.660
8	9.568	34	40.664	60	71.760	86	102.856
9	10.764	35	41.860	61	72.956	87	104.052
10	11.960	36	43.056	62	74.152	88	105.248
11	13.156	37	44.252	63	75.348	89	106.444
12	14.352	38	45.448	64	76.544	90	107.640
13	15.548	39	46.644	65	77.740	91	108.836
14	16.744	40	47.840	66	78.936	92	110.032
15	17.940	41	49.036	67	80.132	93	111.228
16	19.136	42	50.232	68	81.328	94	112.424
17	20.332	43	51.428	69	82.524	95	113.620
18	21.528	44	52.624	70	83.720	96	114.816
19	22.724	45	53.820	71	84.916	97	116.012
20	23.920	46	55.016	72	86.112	98	117.208
21	25.116	47	56.212	73	87.308	99	118.404
22	26.312	48	57.408	74	88.504	100	119.600
23	27.508	49	58.604	75	89.700	200	239.200
24	28.704	50	59.800	76	90.896	400	478.400
25	29.900	51	60.996	77	92.092	600	717.600
26	31.096	52	62.192	78	93.288	1000	1196.00

VOLUME CONVERSION TABLE
CUBIC YARDS TO CUBIC METRES

C.yd.	C.m.	C.yd.	C.m.	C.yd.	C.m.	C.yd.	C.m.
1	0.765	27	20.643	53	40.522	79	60.399
2	1.529	28	21.407	54	41.286	80	61.164
3	2.294	29	22.172	55	42.050	81	61.929
4	3.058	30	22.937	56	42.815	82	62.693
5	3.823	31	23.702	57	43.579	83	63.458
6	4.587	32	24.466	58	44.344	84	64.222
7	5.352	33	25.231	59	45.108	85	64.987
8	6.116	34	25.995	60	45.873	86	65.752
9	6.881	35	26.760	61	46.638	87	66.516
10	7.646	36	27.524	62	47.402	88	67.281
11	8.411	37	28.289	63	48.167	89	68.045
12	9.175	38	29.053	64	48.931	90	68.810
13	9.940	39	29.818	65	49.696	91	69.575
14	10.704	40	30.582	66	50.461	92	70.339
15	11.469	41	31.347	67	51.225	93	71.104
16	12.233	42	32.111	68	51.990	94	71.868
17	12.998	43	32.876	69	52.754	95	72.632
18	13.762	44	33.640	70	53.519	96	73.397
19	14.527	45	34.405	71	54.284	97	74.161
20	15.291	46	35.169	72	55.048	98	74.926
21	16.056	47	35.934	73	55.813	99	75.690
22	16.820	48	36.698	74	56.577	100	76.455
23	17.585	49	37.463	75	57.341	200	152.910
24	18.349	50	38.228	76	58.106	400	305.820
25	19.114	51	38.993	77	58.870	600	458.730
26	19.878	52	39.757	78	59.635	1000	764.550

VOLUME CONVERSION TABLE
CUBIC METRES TO CUBIC YARDS

C.m.	C.yd.	C.m.	C.yd.	C.m.	C.yd.	C.m.	C.yd.
1	1.308	27	35.315	53	69.322	79	103.328
2	2.616	28	36.623	54	70.630	80	104.636
3	3.924	29	37.931	55	71.937	81	105.944
4	5.232	30	39.239	56	73.245	82	107.252
5	6.540	31	40.547	57	74.553	83	108.560
6	7.848	32	41.854	58	75.861	84	109.868
7	9.156	33	43.162	59	77.169	85	111.176
8	10.464	34	44.470	60	78.477	86	112.484
9	11.772	35	45.778	61	79.785	87	113.792
10	13.080	36	47.086	62	81.093	88	115.100
11	14.388	37	48.394	63	82.401	89	116.408
12	15.695	38	49.702	64	83.709	90	117.716
13	17.003	39	51.010	65	85.017	91	119.024
14	18.311	40	52.318	66	86.325	92	120.332
15	19.619	41	53.626	67	87.633	93	121.640
16	20.927	42	54.934	68	88.941	94	122.948
17	22.235	43	56.242	69	90.249	95	124.255
18	23.543	44	57.550	70	91.557	96	125.563
19	24.851	45	58.858	71	92.865	97	126.871
20	26.159	46	60.166	72	94.173	98	128.179
21	27.467	47	61.474	73	95.481	99	129.487
22	28.775	48	62.782	74	96.789	100	130.795
23	30.083	49	64.090	75	98.096	200	261.590
24	31.391	50	65.398	76	99.404	400	523.180
25	32.699	51	66.706	77	100.712	600	784.770
26	34.007	52	68.014	78	102.020	1000	1307.950

CAPACITY CONVERSION TABLE
PINTS TO LITRES

Pints	Litres	Pints	Litres	Pints	Litres	Pints	Litres
1	0.568	27	15.342	53	30.117	79	44.891
2	1.136	28	15.911	54	30.685	80	45.459
3	1.705	29	16.479	55	31.253	81	46.027
4	2.273	30	17.047	56	31.821	82	46.595
5	2.841	31	17.615	57	32.389	83	47.164
6	3.409	32	18.184	58	32.958	84	47.732
7	3.978	33	18.752	59	33.526	85	48.300
8	4.546	34	19.320	60	34.094	86	48.868
9	5.114	35	19.888	61	34.662	87	49.436
10	5.682	36	20.457	62	35.230	88	50.005
11	6.250	37	21.025	63	35.799	89	50.573
12	6.819	38	21.593	64	36.367	90	51.142
13	7.387	39	22.161	65	36.936	91	51.710
14	7.955	40	22.730	66	37.504	92	52.278
15	8.523	41	23.298	67	38.072	93	52.847
16	9.092	42	23.866	68	38.641	94	53.415
17	9.660	43	24.434	69	39.209	95	53.983
18	10.228	44	25.003	70	39.777	96	54.551
19	10.796	45	25.571	71	40.345	97	55.119
20	11.365	46	26.139	72	40.913	98	55.688
21	11.933	47	26.707	73	41.482	99	56.256
22	12.501	48	27.276	74	42.050	100	56.824
23	13.069	49	27.844	75	42.618	200	113.648
24	13.638	50	28.412	76	43.186	400	227.296
25	14.206	51	28.980	77	43.754	600	340.944
26	14.774	52	29.548	78	44.323	1000	568.240

CAPACITY CONVERSION TABLE
LITRES TO PINTS

Litres	Pints	Litres	Pints	Litres	Pints	Litres	Pints
1	1.760	27	47.515	53	93.270	79	139.025
2	3.520	28	49.274	54	95.030	80	140.784
3	5.279	29	51.034	55	96.789	81	142.544
4	7.039	30	52.794	56	98.549	82	144.304
5	8.799	31	54.554	57	100.309	83	146.064
6	10.559	32	56.314	58	102.069	84	147.824
7	12.319	33	58.074	59	103.829	85	149.583
8	14.078	34	59.833	60	105.588	86	151.343
9	15.838	35	61.593	61	107.348	87	153.103
10	17.598	36	63.353	62	109.108	88	154.863
11	19.358	37	65.113	63	110.868	89	156.623
12	21.118	38	66.872	64	112.628	90	158.382
13	22.878	39	68.632	65	114.387	91	160.142
14	24.637	40	70.392	66	116.147	92	161.902
15	26.397	41	72.152	67	117.907	93	163.662
16	28.157	42	73.912	68	119.667	94	165.422
17	29.917	43	75.672	69	121.427	95	167.181
18	31.676	44	77.431	70	123.186	96	168.941
19	33.436	45	79.191	71	124.946	97	170.701
20	35.196	46	80.951	72	126.706	98	172.461
21	36.956	47	82.711	73	128.466	99	174.221
22	38.716	48	84.470	74	130.226	100	175.980
23	40.476	49	86.230	75	131.985	200	351.960
24	42.235	50	87.990	76	133.745	400	703.920
25	43.995	51	89.750	77	135.505	600	1055.880
26	45.755	52	91.510	78	137.265	1000	1759.800

WEIGHT CONVERSION TABLE
POUNDS TO KILOGRAMS

Lb.	Kg.	Lb.	Kg.	Lb.	Kg.	Lb.	Kg.
1	0.454	27	12.247	53	24.041	79	35.833
2	0.907	28	12.701	54	24.494	80	36.287
3	1.361	29	13.155	55	24.948	81	36.741
4	1.814	30	13.608	56	25.402	82	37.194
5	2.268	31	14.062	57	25.855	83	37.648
6	2.722	32	14.515	58	26.309	84	38.101
7	3.175	33	14.969	59	26.762	85	38.555
8	3.629	34	15.422	60	27.216	86	39.009
9	4.082	35	15.876	61	27.670	87	39.462
10	4.536	36	16.329	62	28.123	88	39.916
11	4.989	37	16.783	63	28.577	89	40.369
12	5.443	38	17.236	64	29.030	90	40.823
13	5.896	39	17.690	65	29.483	91	41.277
14	6.350	40	18.144	66	29.937	92	41.730
15	6.803	41	18.598	67	30.390	93	42.184
16	7.257	42	19.051	68	30.844	94	42.637
17	7.711	43	19.505	69	31.297	95	43.091
18	8.165	44	19.958	70	31.751	96	43.545
19	8.619	45	20.412	71	32.205	97	43.998
20	9.072	46	20.865	72	32.658	98	44.452
21	9.526	47	21.319	73	33.112	99	44.905
22	9.979	48	21.772	74	33.565	100	45.359
23	10.433	49	22.226	75	34.019	200	90.718
24	10.886	50	22.680	76	34.473	400	181.436
25	11.340	51	23.134	77	34.926	600	272.154
26	11.793	52	23.587	78	35.380	1000	453.590

WEIGHT CONVERSION TABLE
KILOGRAMS TO POUNDS

Kg.	Lb.	Kg.	Lb.	Kg.	Lb.	Kg.	Lb.
1	2.205	27	59.525	53	116.845	79	174.165
2	4.409	28	61.729	54	119.049	80	176.370
3	6.614	29	63.934	55	121.254	81	178.575
4	8.818	30	66.139	56	123.459	82	180.780
5	11.023	31	68.344	57	125.664	83	182.984
6	13.228	32	70.548	58	127.868	84	185.188
7	15.432	33	72.753	59	130.072	85	187.393
8	17.637	34	74.957	60	132.277	86	189.598
9	19.842	35	77.162	61	134.482	87	191.803
10	22.046	36	79.366	62	136.687	88	194.007
11	24.251	37	81.571	63	138.891	89	196.211
12	26.455	38	83.776	64	141.095	90	198.416
13	28.660	39	85.981	65	143.300	91	200.621
14	30.865	40	88.185	66	145.505	92	202.826
15	33.070	41	90.390	67	147.710	93	205.030
16	35.274	42	92.594	68	149.914	94	207.234
17	37.479	43	94.799	69	152.118	95	209.439
18	39.683	44	97.003	70	154.324	96	211.644
19	41.888	45	99.208	71	156.529	97	213.849
20	44.092	46	101.413	72	158.734	98	216.053
21	46.297	47	103.618	73	160.938	99	218.257
22	48.502	48	105.822	74	163.142	100	220.462
23	50.707	49	108.027	75	165.347	200	440.924
24	52.911	50	110.231	76	167.552	400	881.848
25	55.116	51	112.436	77	169.757	600	1322.772
26	57.320	52	114.641	78	171.961	1000	2204.620

MULTIPLICATION SQUARE

1	2	3	4	5	6	7	8	9	10	11	12	13	14	15	16	17	18
2	4	6	8	10	12	14	16	18	20	22	24	26	28	30	32	34	36
3	6	9	12	15	18	21	24	27	30	33	36	39	42	45	48	51	54
4	8	12	16	20	24	28	32	36	40	44	48	52	56	60	64	68	72
5	10	15	20	25	30	35	40	45	50	55	60	65	70	75	80	85	90
6	12	18	24	30	36	42	48	54	60	66	72	78	84	90	96	102	108
7	14	21	28	35	42	49	56	63	70	77	84	91	98	105	112	119	126
8	16	24	32	40	48	56	64	72	80	88	96	104	112	120	128	136	144
9	18	27	36	45	54	63	72	81	90	99	108	117	126	135	144	153	162
10	20	30	40	50	60	70	80	90	100	110	120	130	140	150	160	170	180
11	22	33	44	55	66	77	88	99	110	121	132	143	154	165	176	187	198
12	24	36	48	60	72	84	96	108	120	132	144	156	168	180	192	204	216
13	26	39	52	65	78	91	104	117	130	143	156	169	182	195	208	221	234
14	28	42	56	70	84	98	112	126	140	154	168	182	196	210	224	238	252
15	30	45	60	75	90	105	120	135	150	165	180	195	210	225	240	255	270
16	32	48	64	80	96	112	128	144	160	176	192	208	224	240	256	272	288
17	34	51	68	85	102	119	136	153	170	187	204	221	238	255	272	289	306
18	36	54	72	90	108	126	144	162	180	198	216	234	252	270	288	306	324

SQUARES, SQUARE ROOTS, CUBES, AND CUBE ROOTS TABLE

Figure	Squares	Square Roots	Cubes	Cube Roots
1	1	1.000	1	1.000
2	4	1.414	8	1.260
3	9	1.732	27	1.442
4	16	2.000	64	1.587
5	25	2.236	125	1.710
6	36	2.449	216	1.817
7	49	2.646	343	1.913
8	64	2.828	512	2.000
9	81	3.000	729	2.080
10	100	3.162	1,000	2.154
11	121	3.316	1,331	2.224
12	144	3.464	1,728	2.289
13	169	3.605	2,197	2.351
14	196	3.741	2,744	2.410
15	225	3.873	3,375	2.466
16	256	4.000	4,096	2.519
17	289	4.123	4,913	2.571
18	324	4.242	5,832	2.620
19	361	4.358	6,859	2.668
20	400	4.472	8,000	2.714
21	441	4.582	9,261	2.758
22	484	4.690	10,648	2.802
23	529	4.795	12,167	2.843
24	576	4.898	13,824	2.884
25	625	5.000	15,625	2.924
26	676	5.099	17,576	2.962
27	729	5.196	19,683	3.000
28	784	5.291	21,952	3.036
29	841	5.385	24,389	3.072
30	900	5.477	27,000	3.107

SQUARES, SQUARE ROOTS, CUBES, AND CUBE ROOTS TABLE (*continued*)

Figure	Squares	Square Roots	Cubes	Cube Roots
31	961	5.567	29,791	3.141
32	1,024	5.656	32,768	3.174
33	1,089	5.744	35,937	3.207
34	1,156	5.830	39,304	3.239
35	1,225	5.916	42,875	3.271
36	1,296	6.000	46,656	3.302
37	1,369	6.083	50,653	3.332
38	1,444	6.164	54,872	3.362
39	1,521	6.245	59,319	3.391
40	1,600	6.325	64,000	3.420
41	1,681	6.403	68,921	3.448
42	1,764	6.481	74,088	3.476
43	1,849	6.557	79,507	3.503
44	1,936	6.633	85,184	3.530
45	2,025	6.708	91,125	3.557
46	2,116	6.782	97,336	3.583
47	2,209	6.856	103,823	3.609
48	2,304	6.928	110,592	3.634
49	2,401	7.000	117,649	3.659
50	2,500	7.071	125,000	3.684
51	2,601	7.141	132,651	3.708
52	2,704	7.211	140,608	3.733
53	2,809	7.280	148,877	3.756
54	2,916	7.348	157,464	3.780
55	3,025	7.416	166,375	3.803
56	3,136	7.483	175,616	3.826
57	3,249	7.550	185,193	3.849
58	3,364	7.616	195,112	3.871
59	3,481	7.681	205,379	3.893
60	3,600	7.746	216,000	3.915